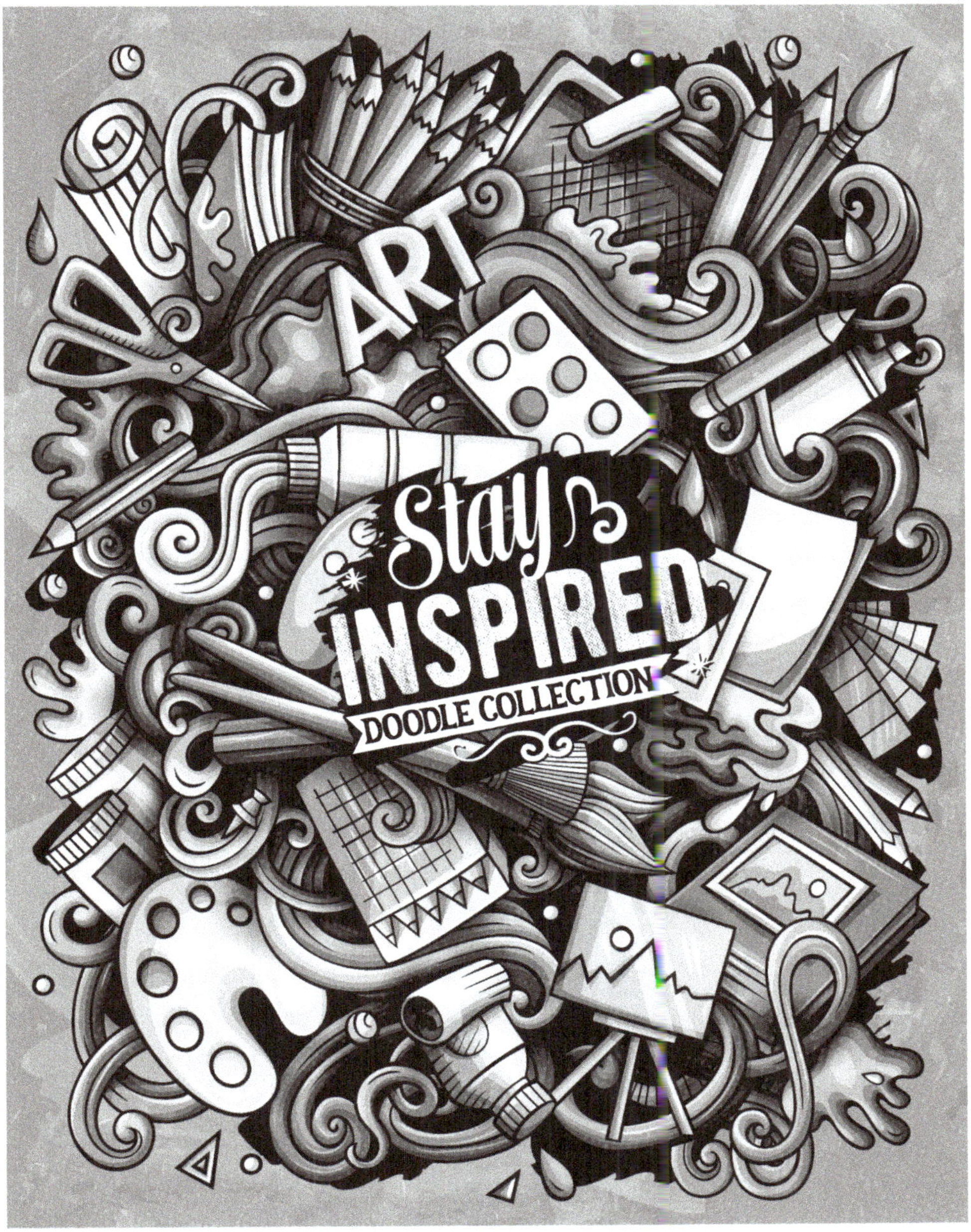

Copyright© 2020 by Saiko Print

All rights reserved. No part of this publication may be reproduced, distributed, or transmitted in any form or by any means, including photocopying, recording, or other electronic methods.

Find us at:

Amazon.com/author/saikoprint

instagram.com/saikoprint

etsy.com/saikoprint

Or you can email us at: saikoprint@mail.com

If you enjoyed using this gratitude journal, please feel free to leave us a positive review! It really helps a lot and means we'll be able to bring more awesome stuff to you in the future!

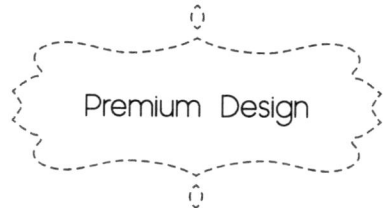

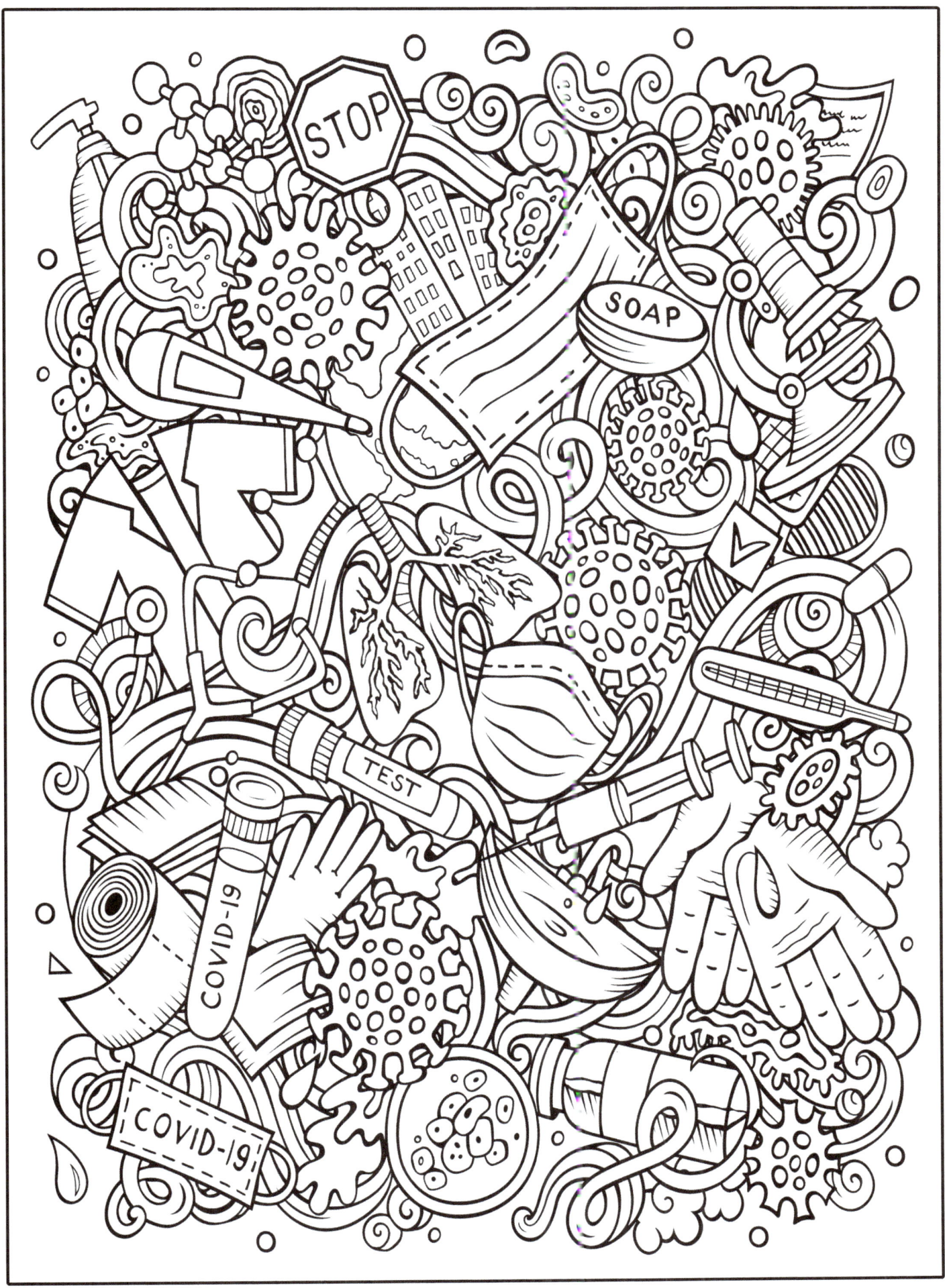

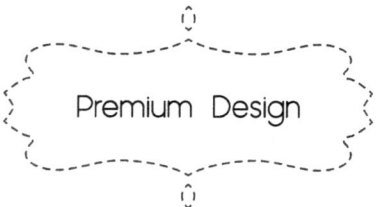

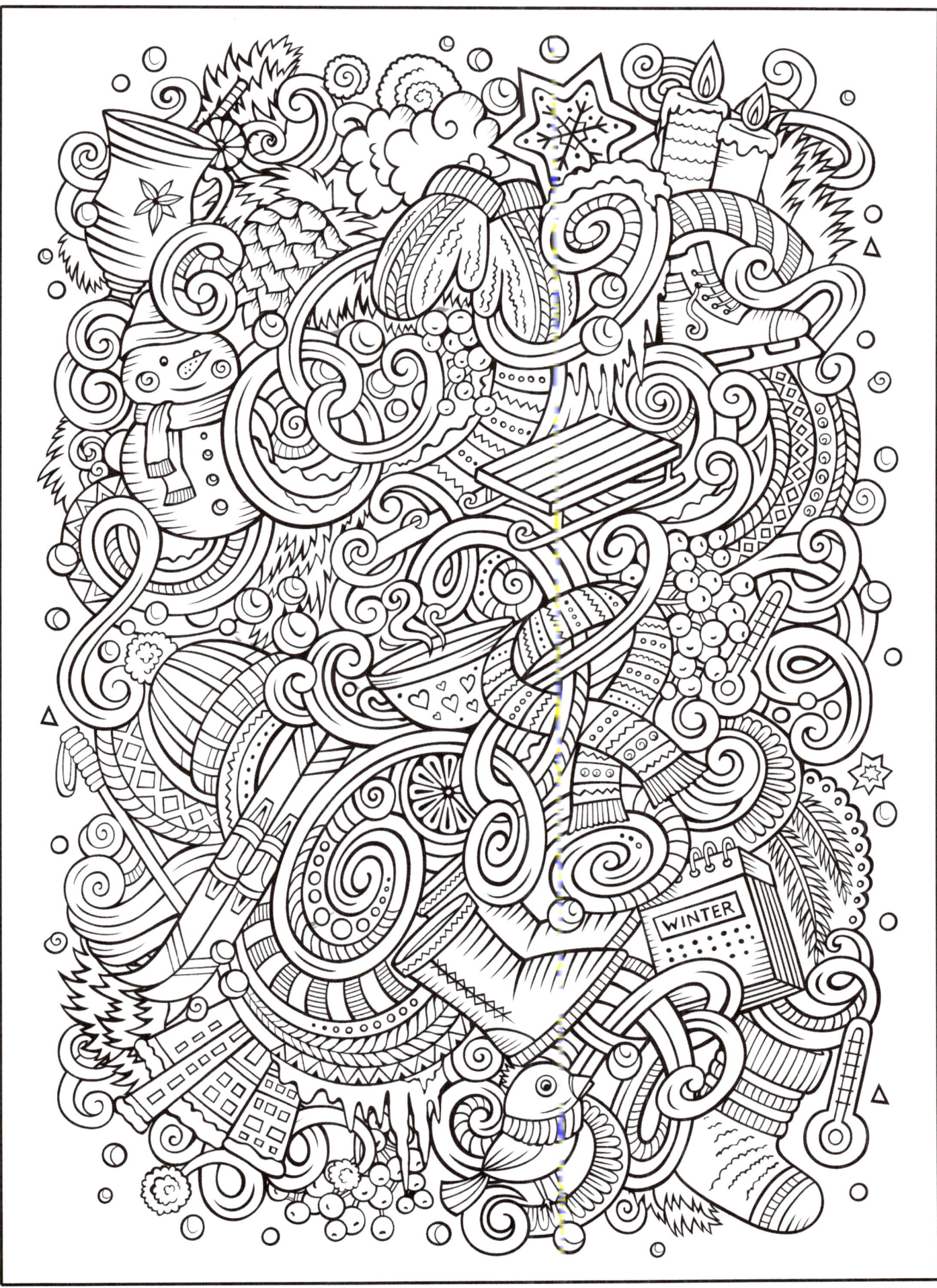

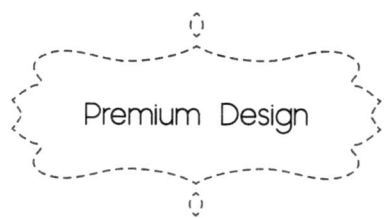
Premium Design

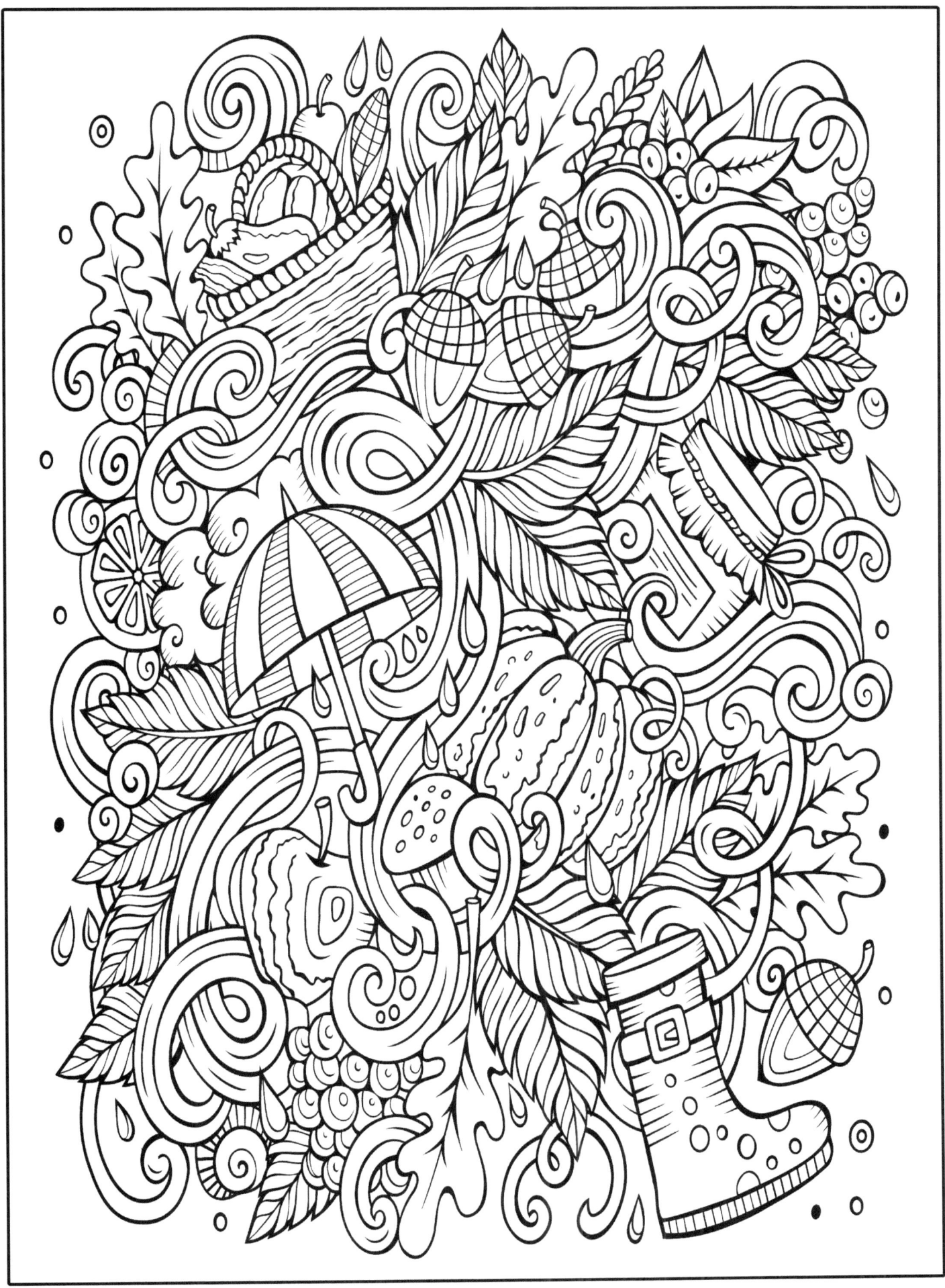

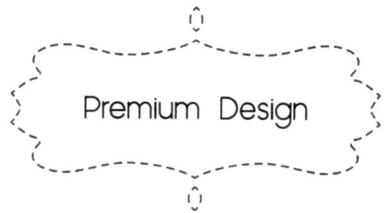

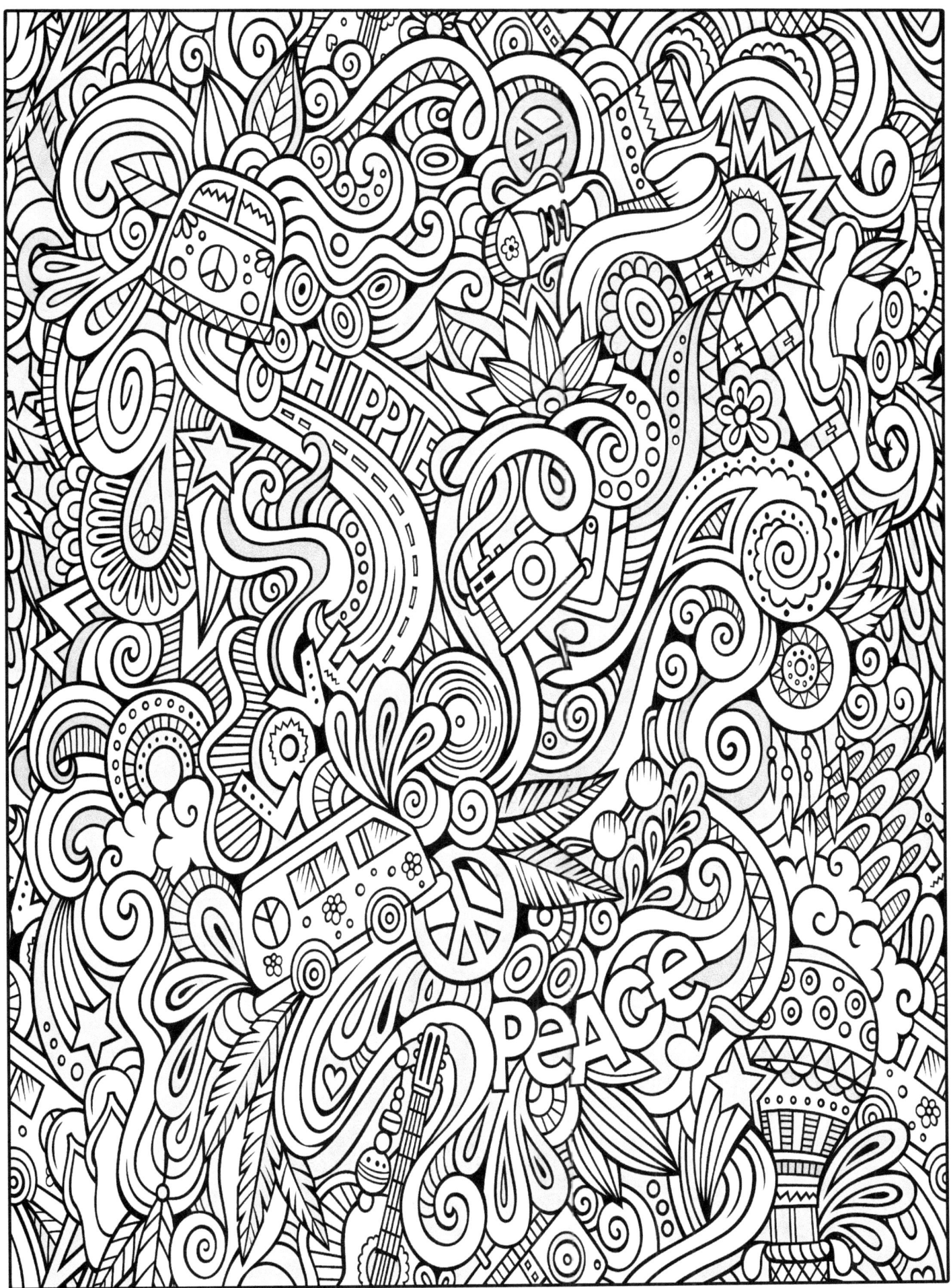

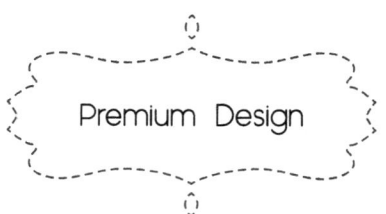

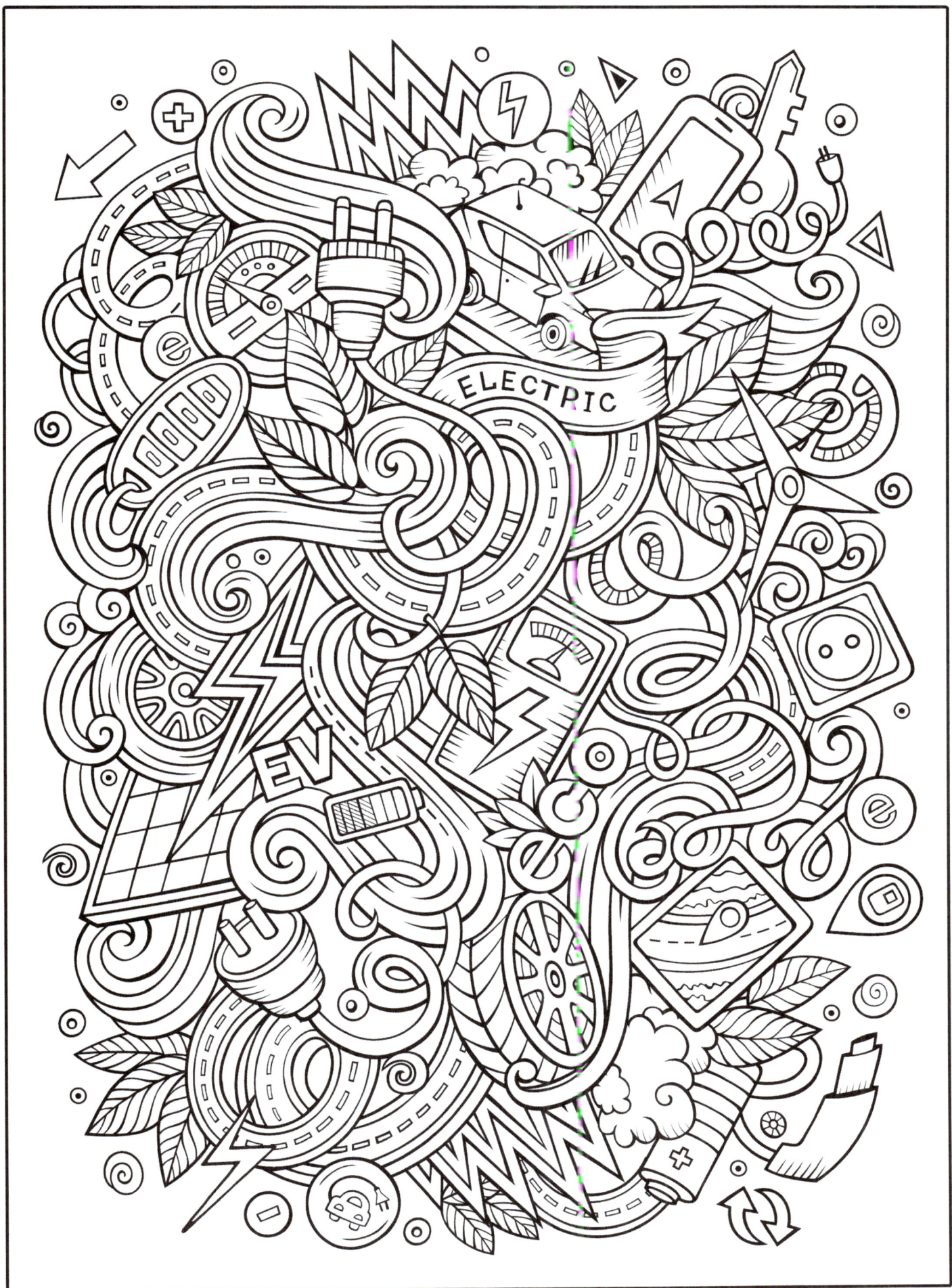

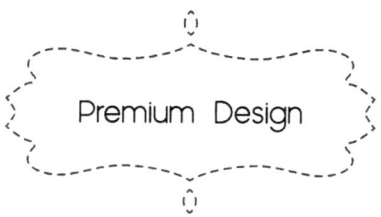

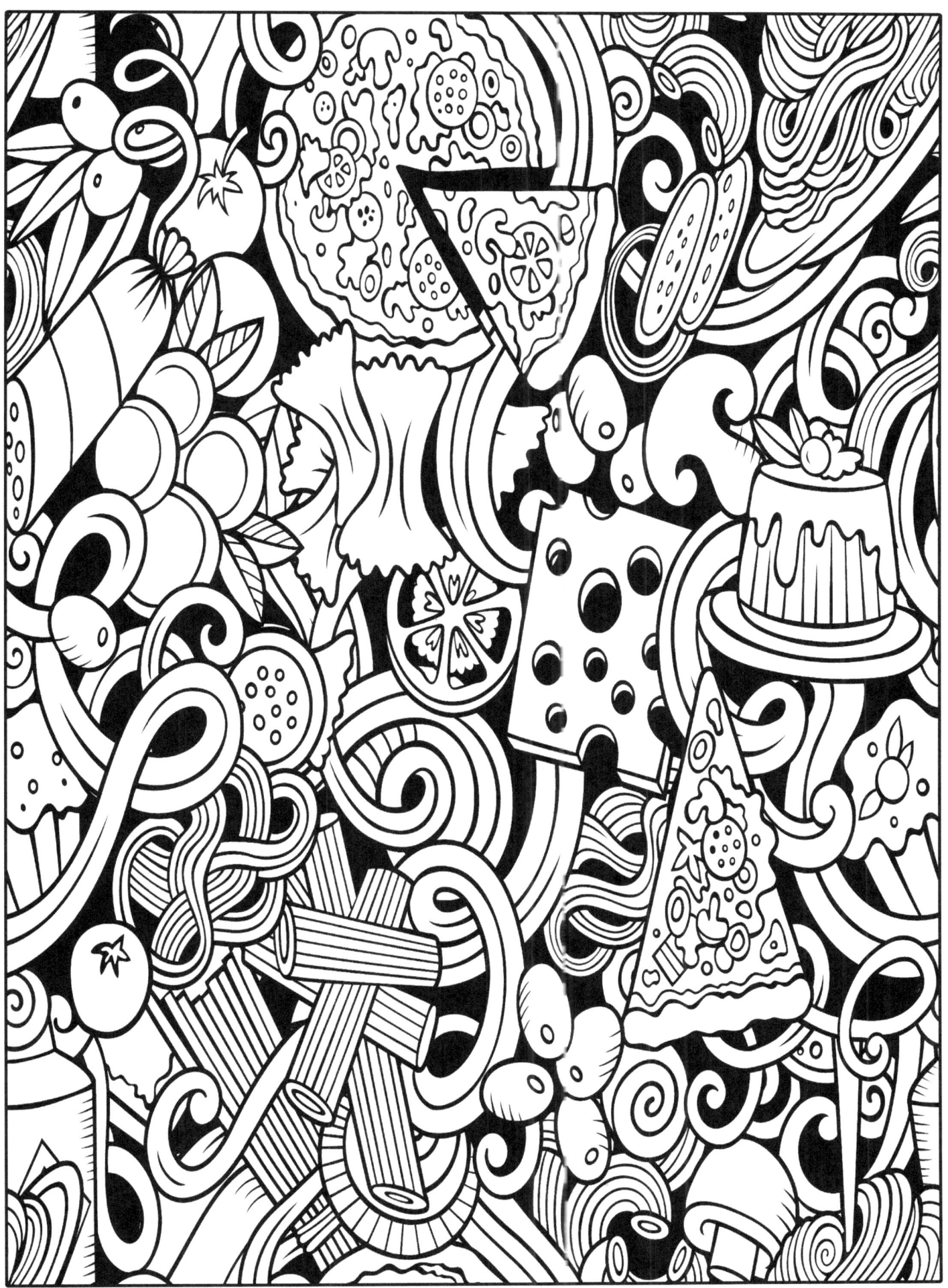

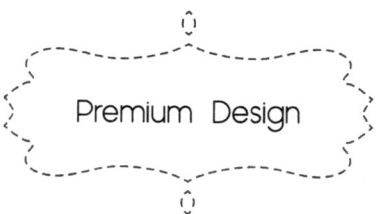

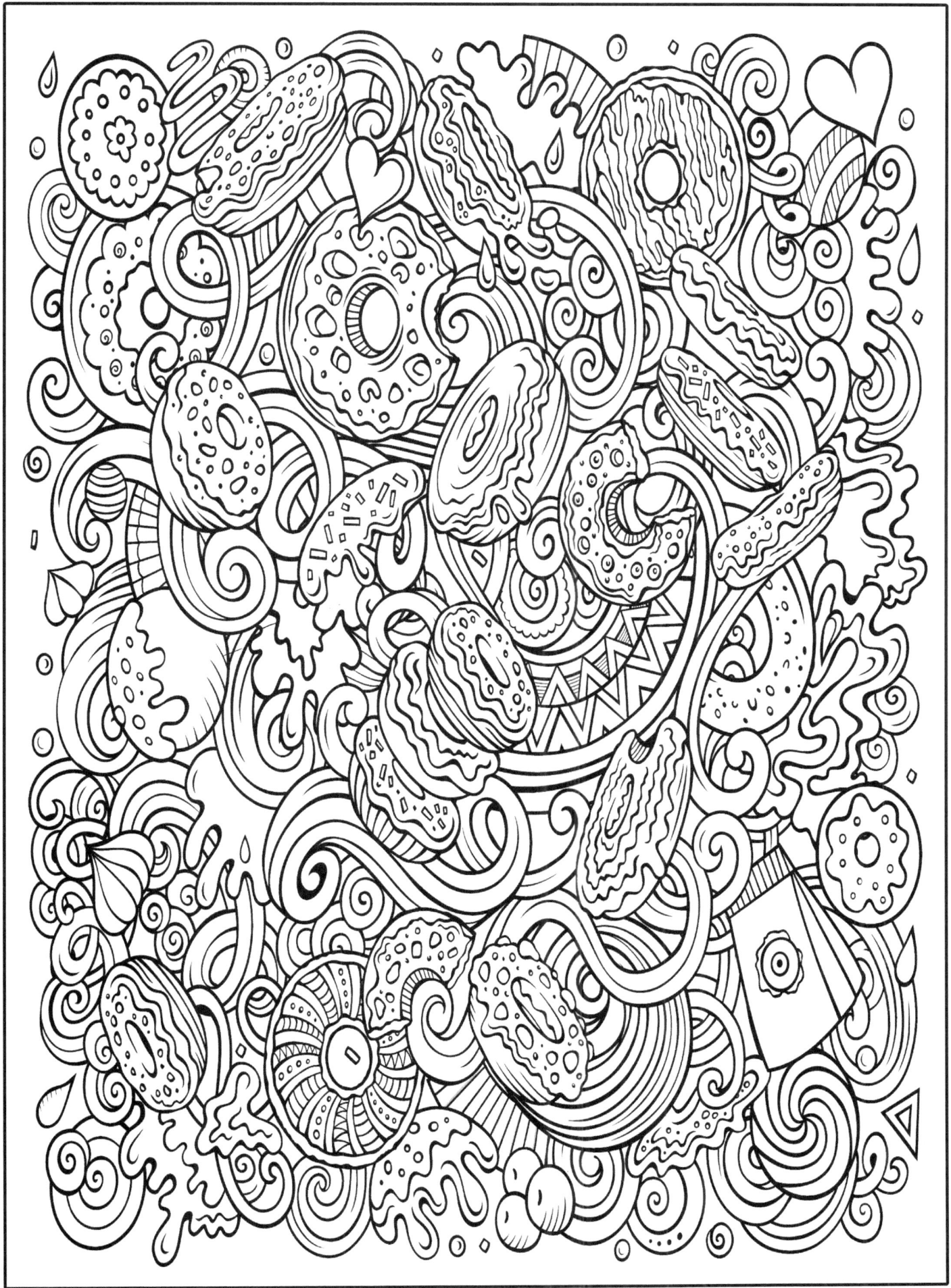

Premium Design

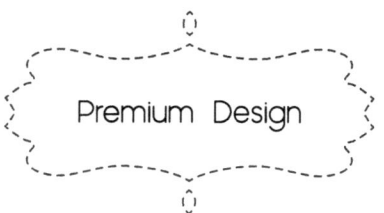

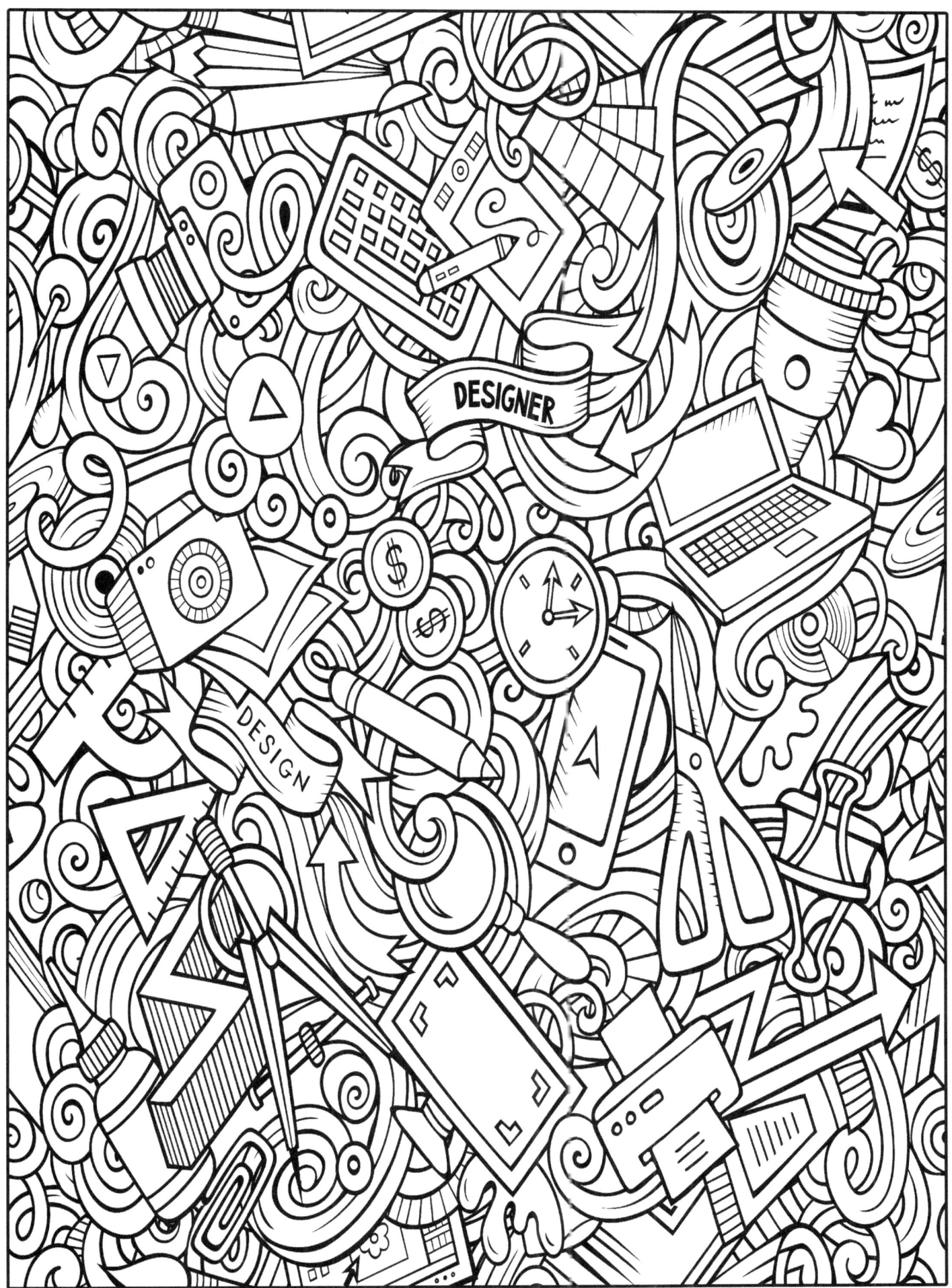

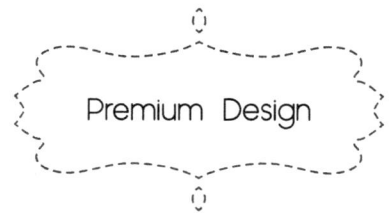

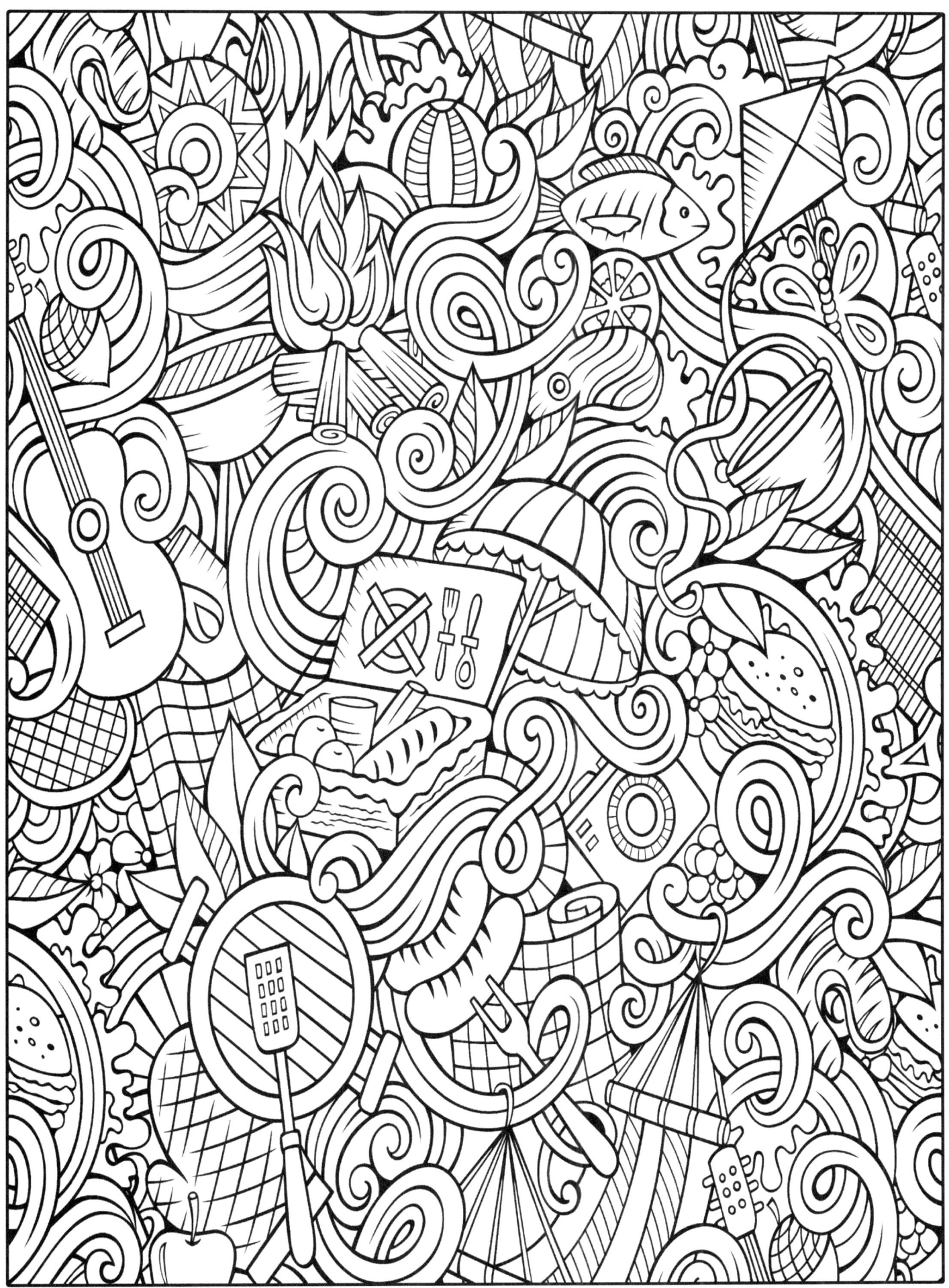

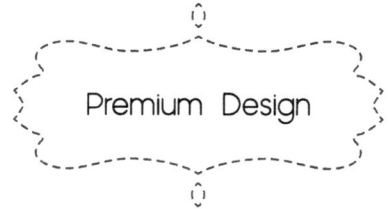

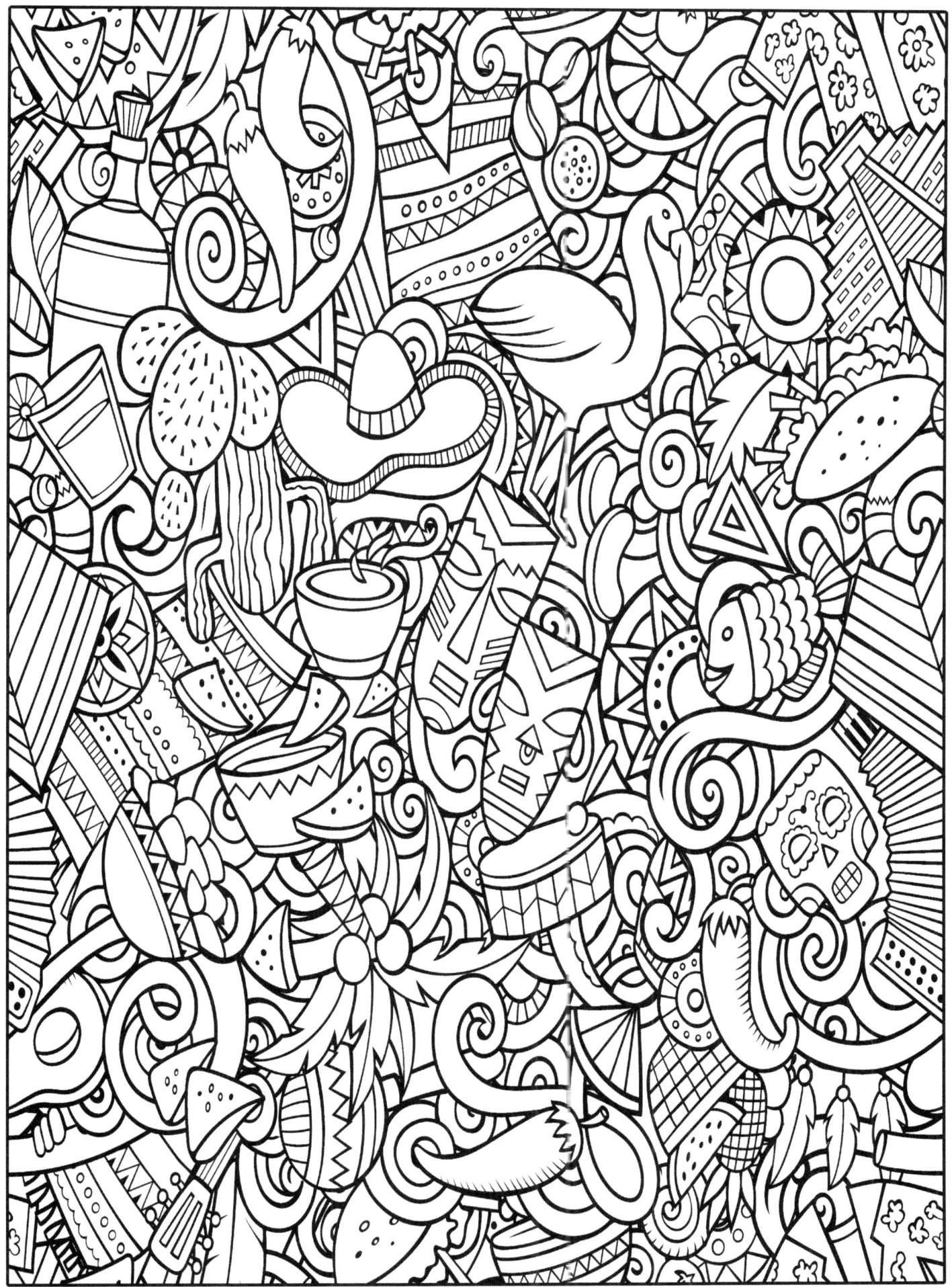

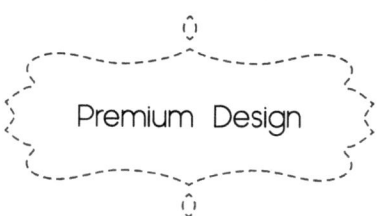

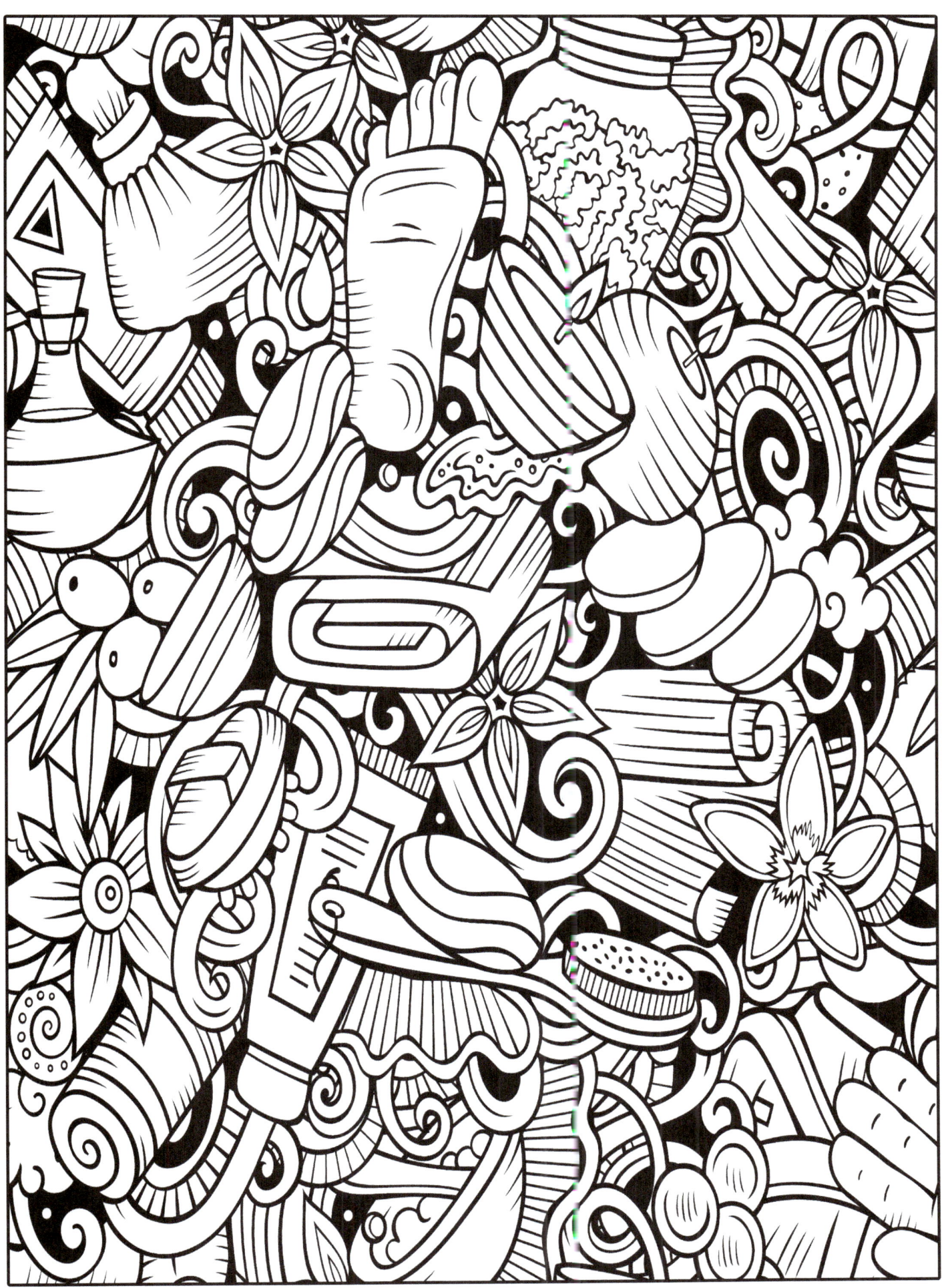

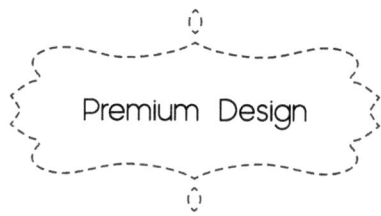

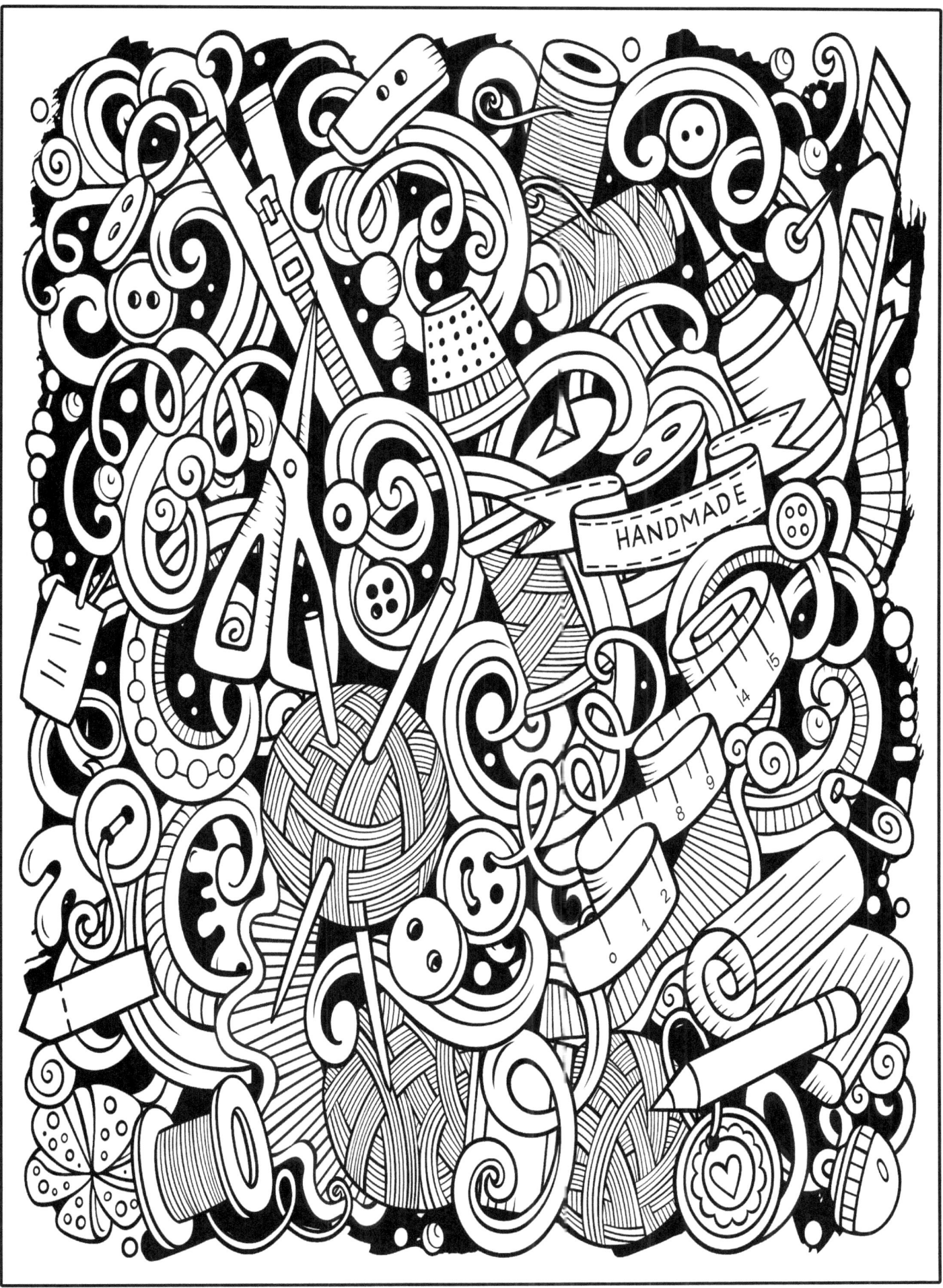

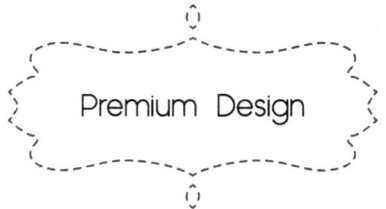

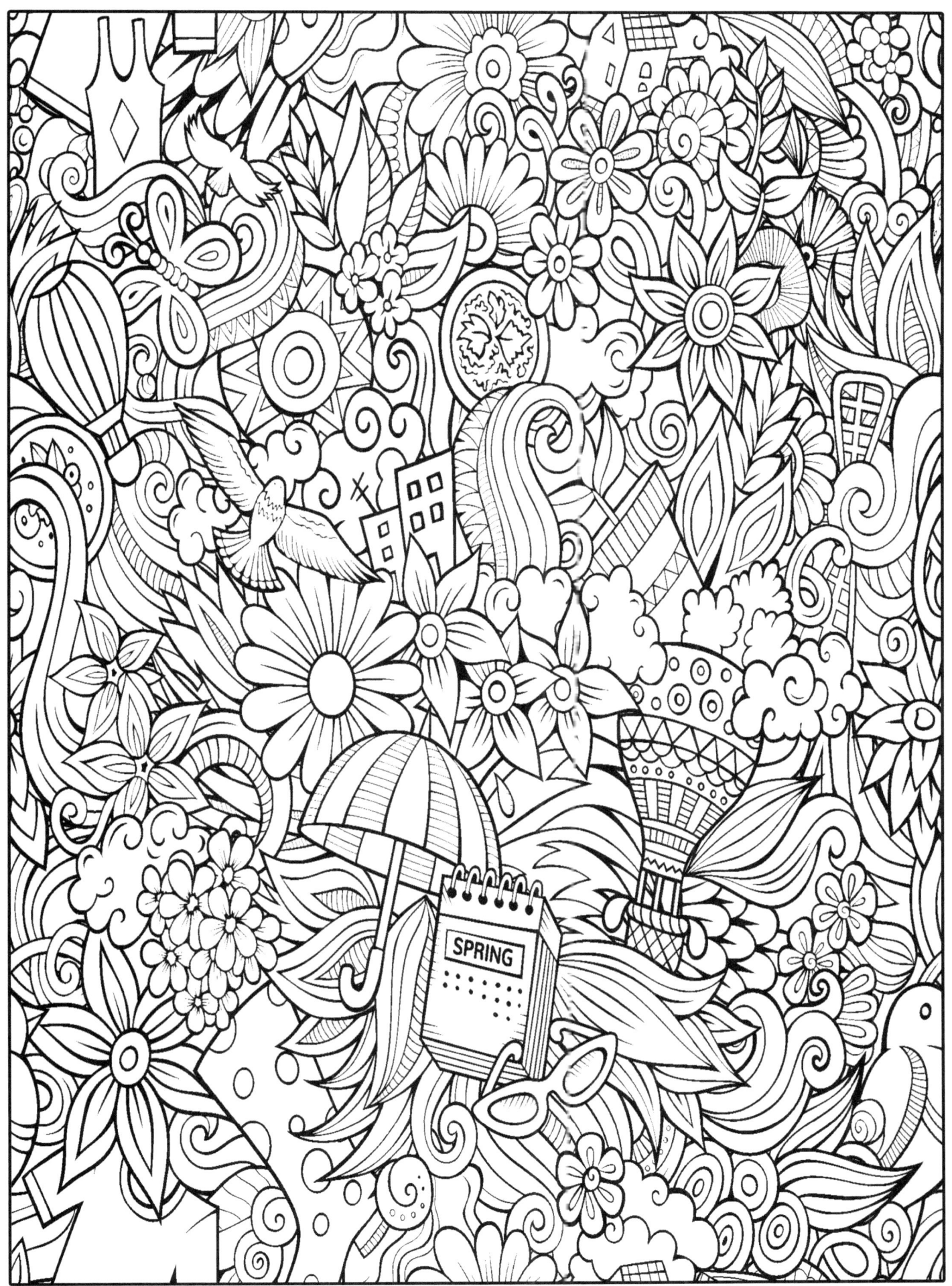

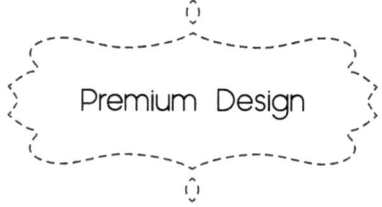

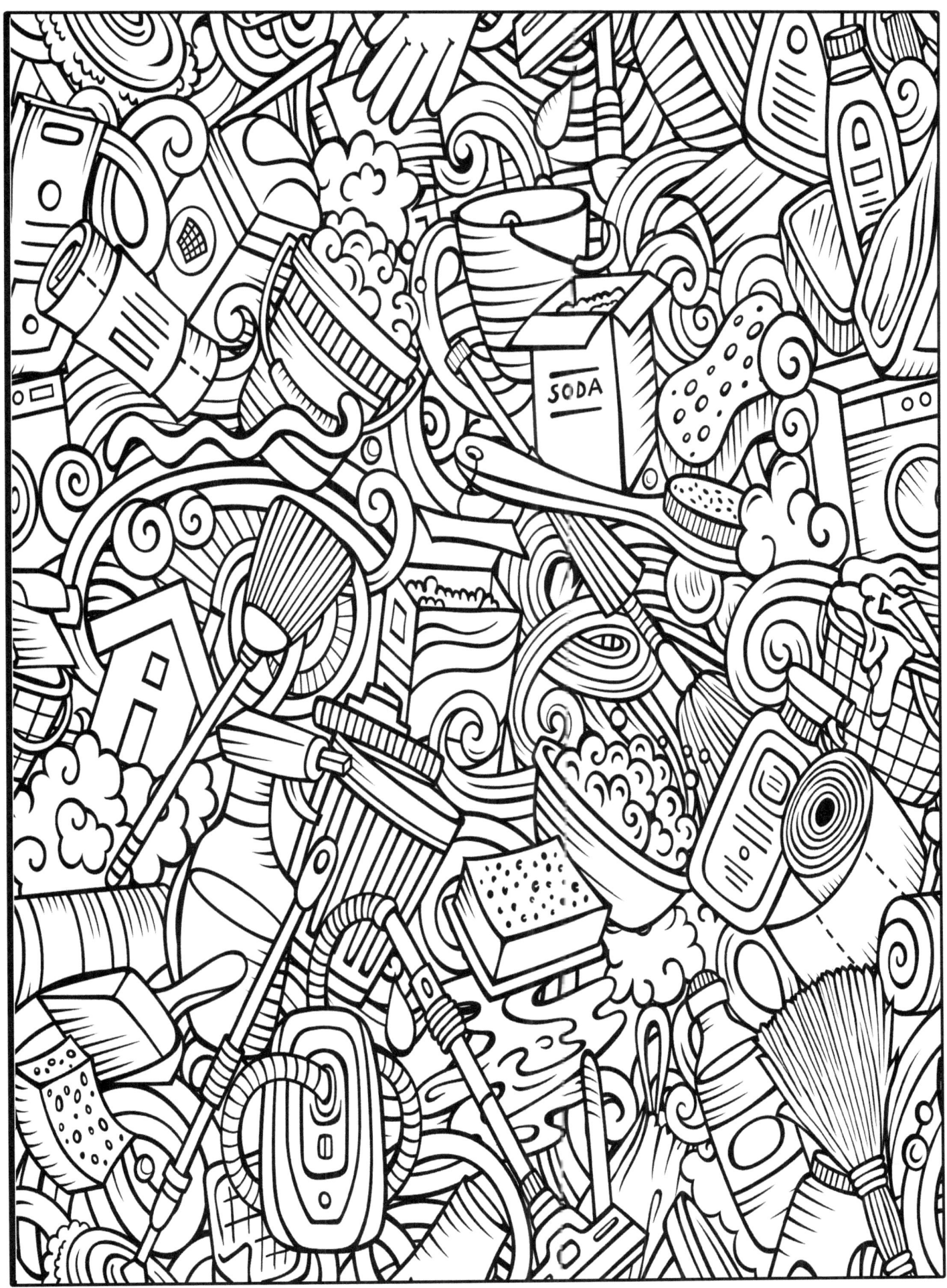

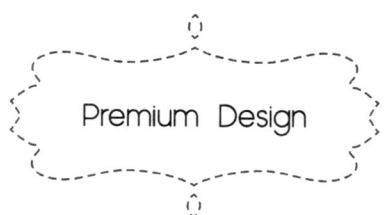

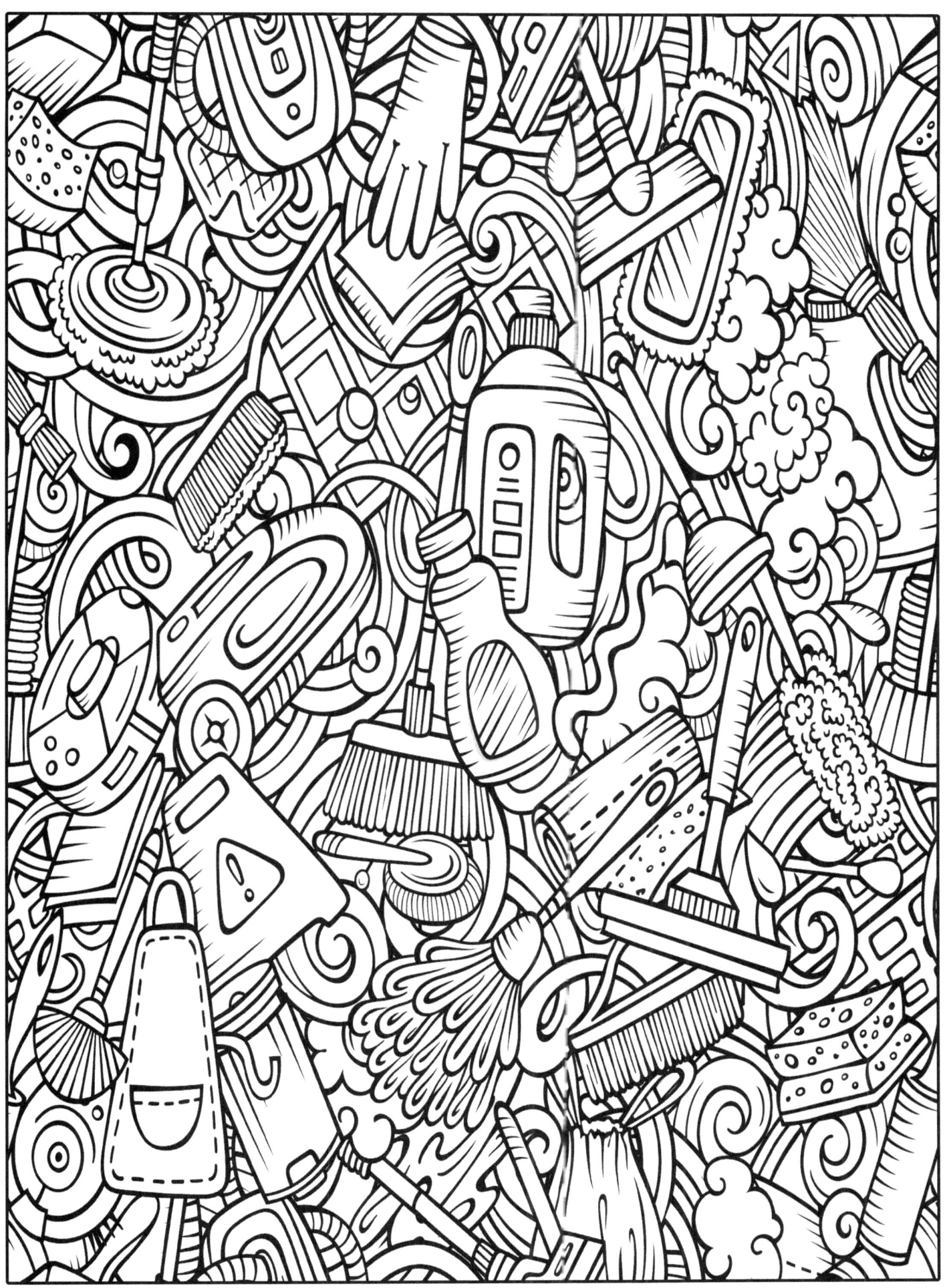

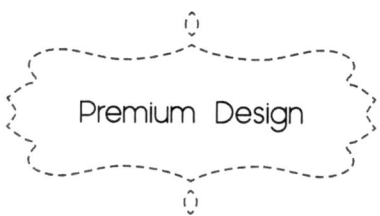

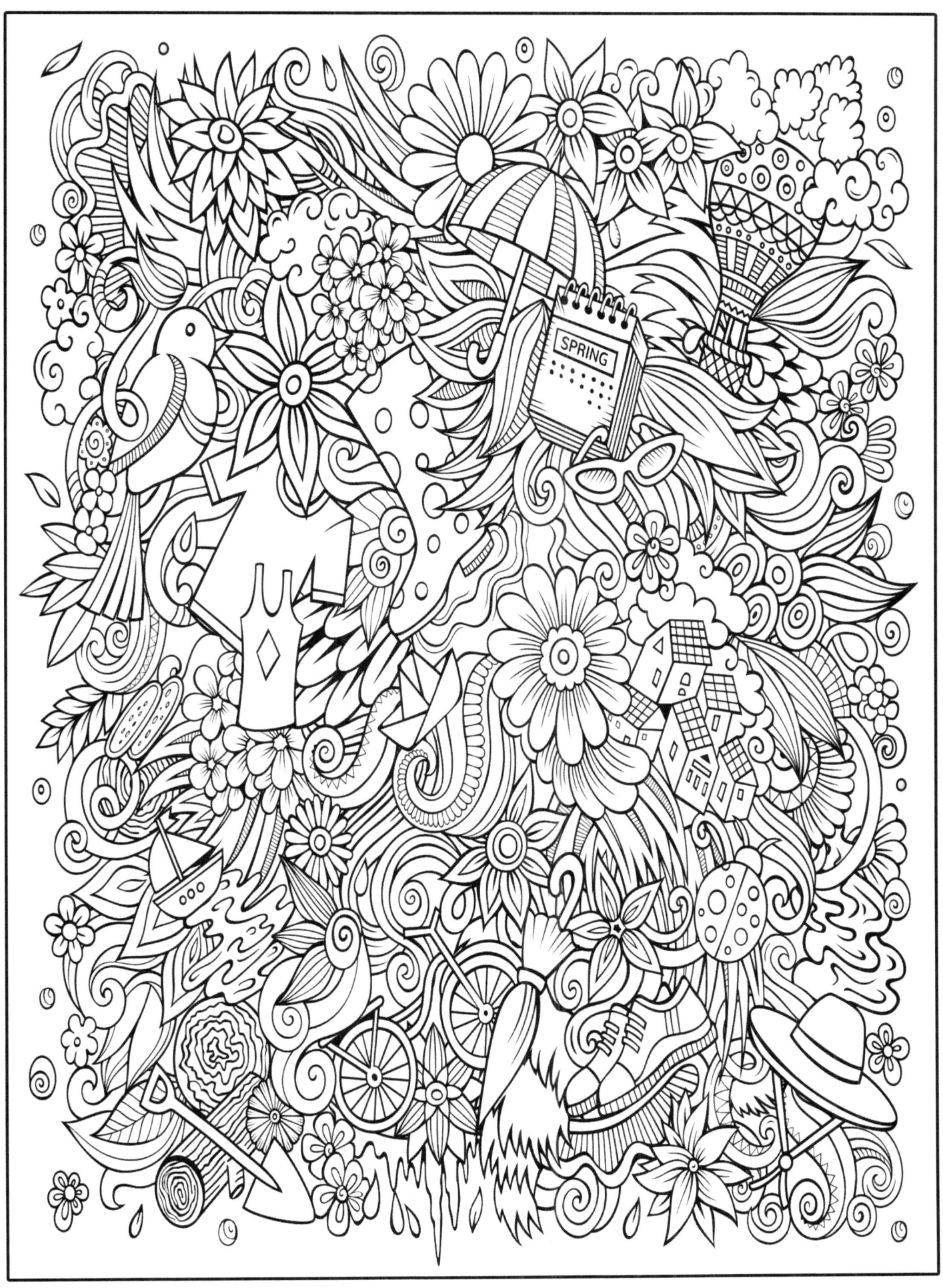

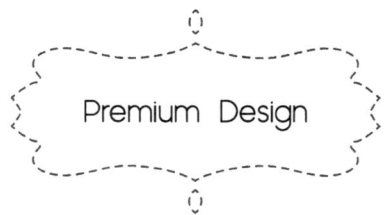

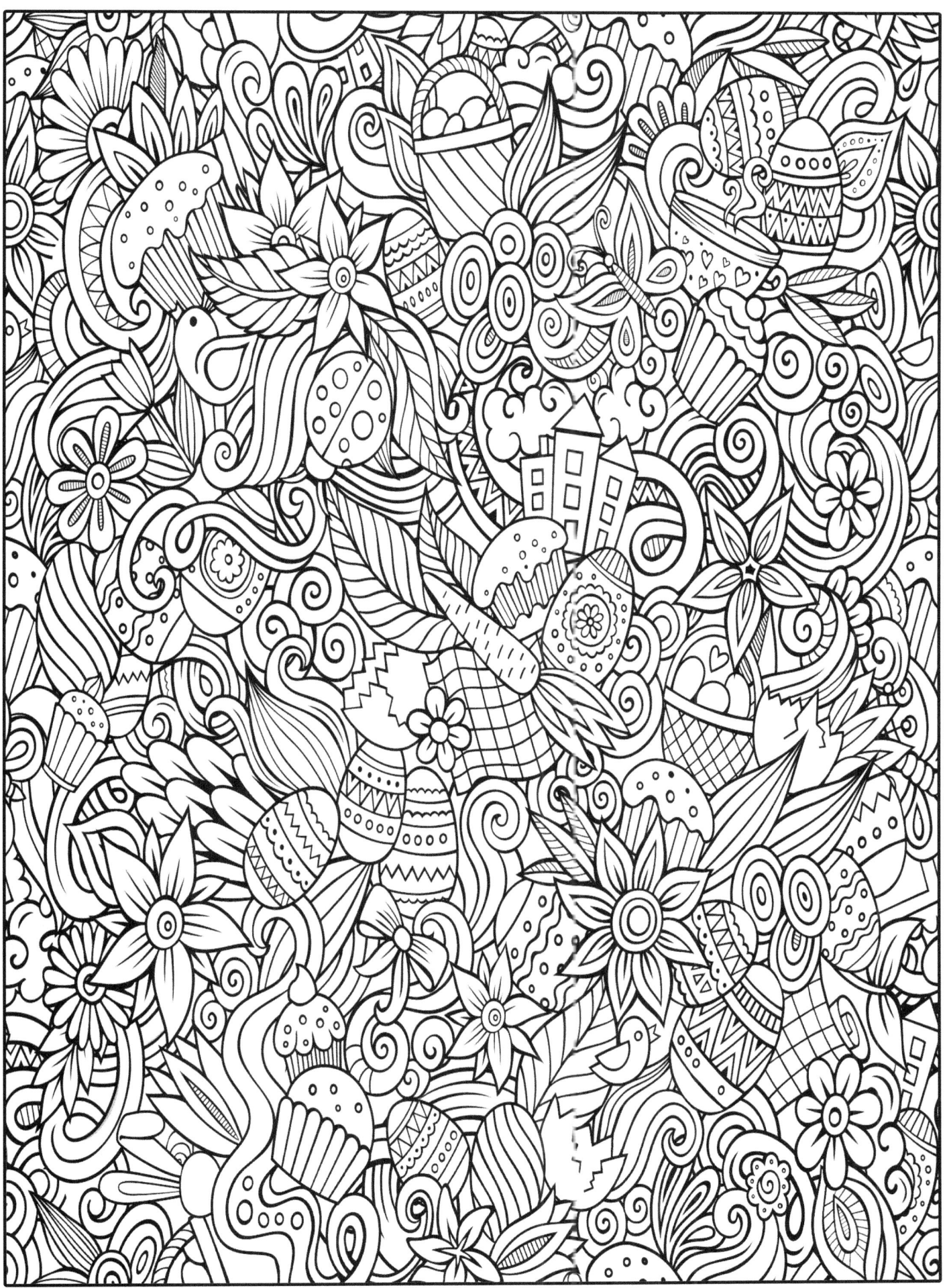

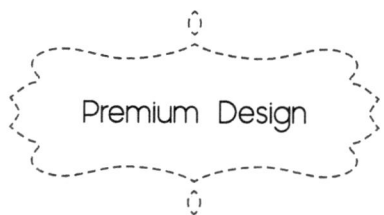

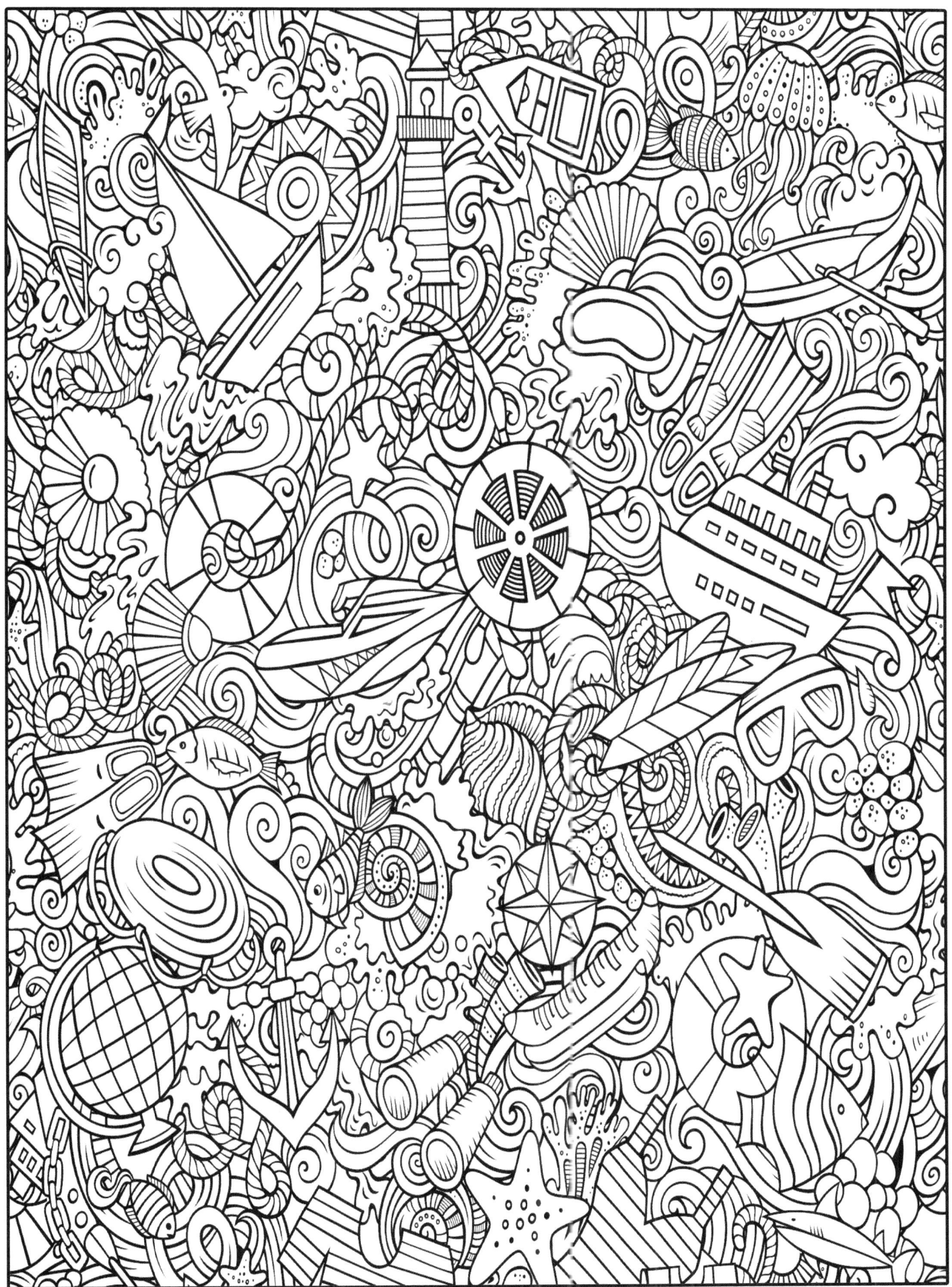

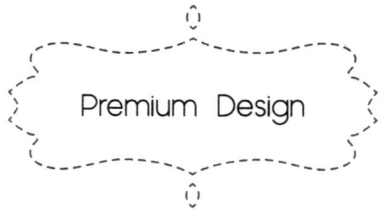

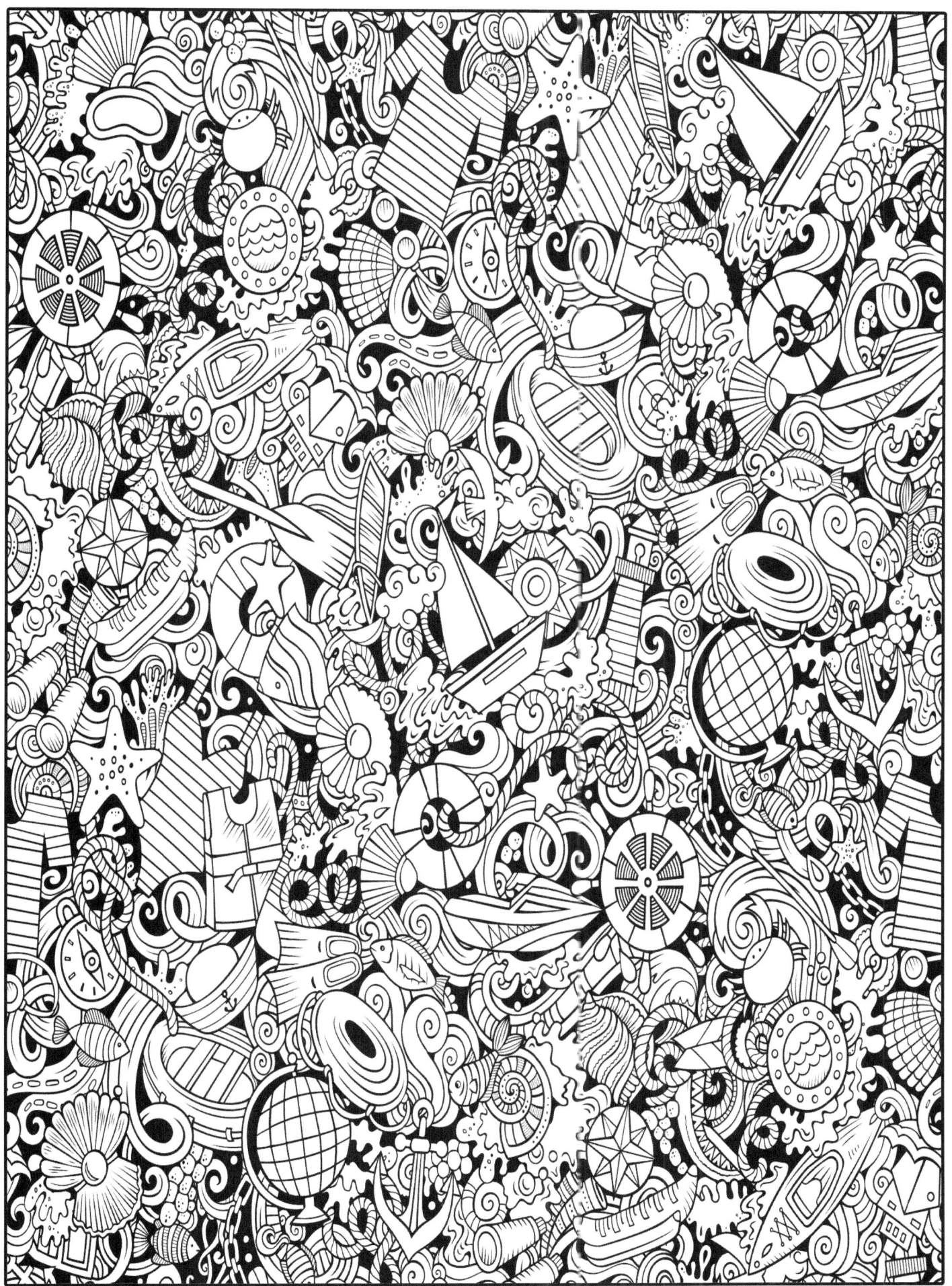

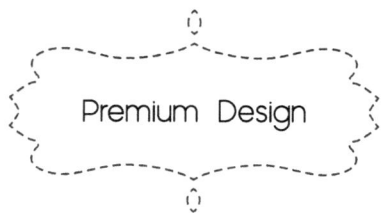

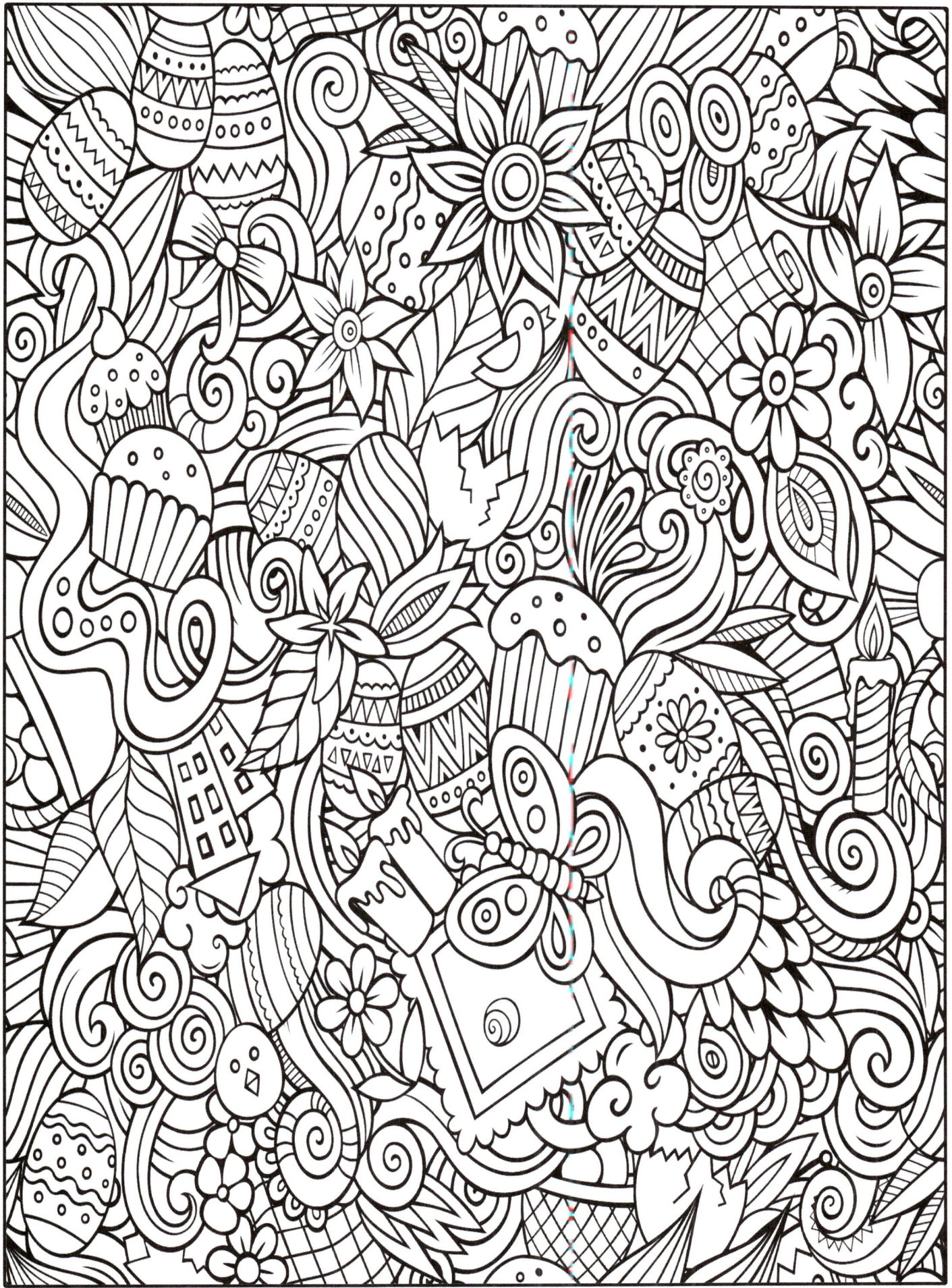

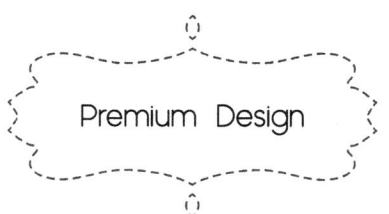

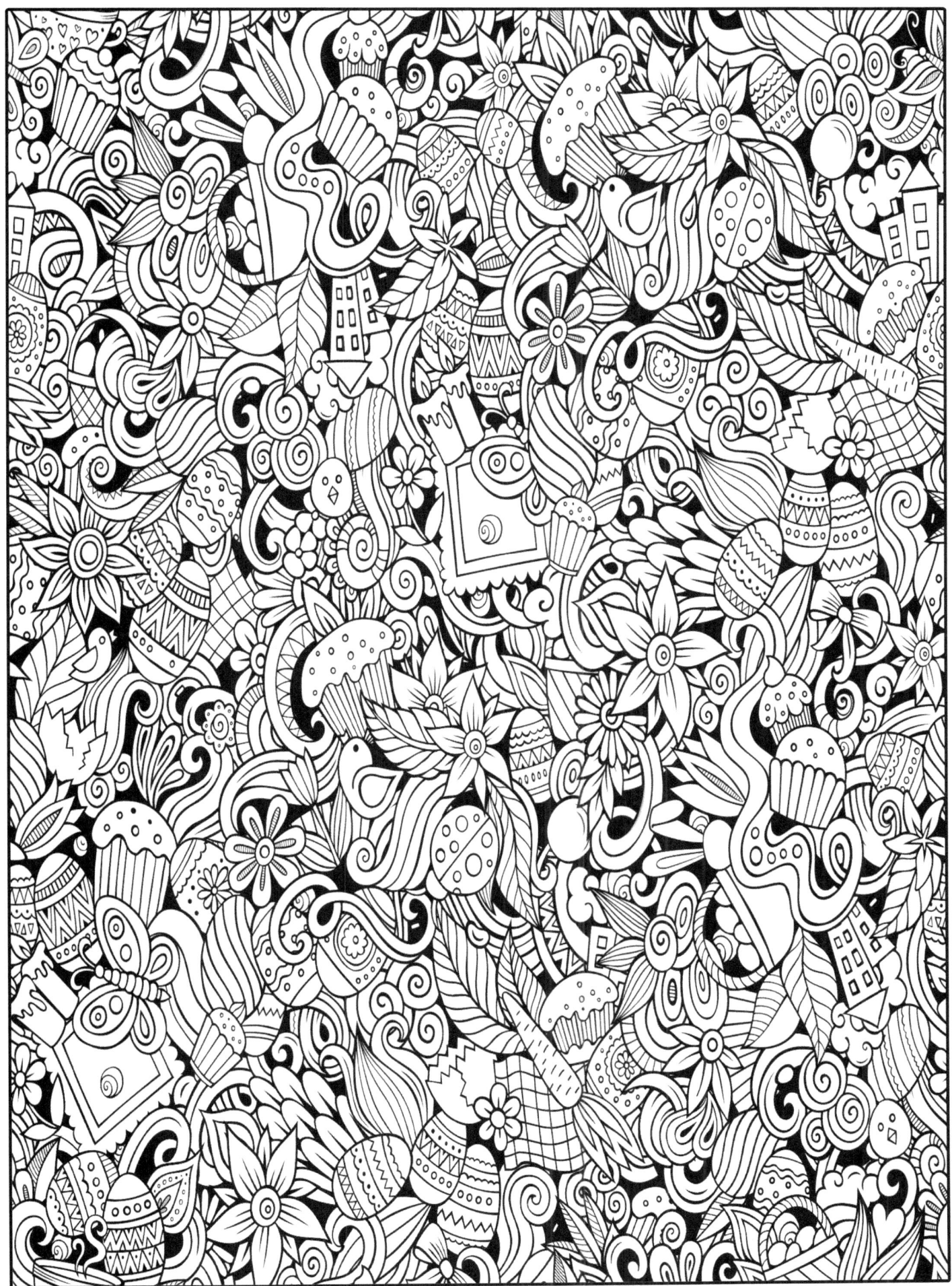

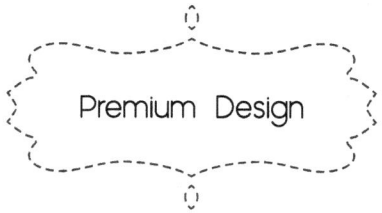

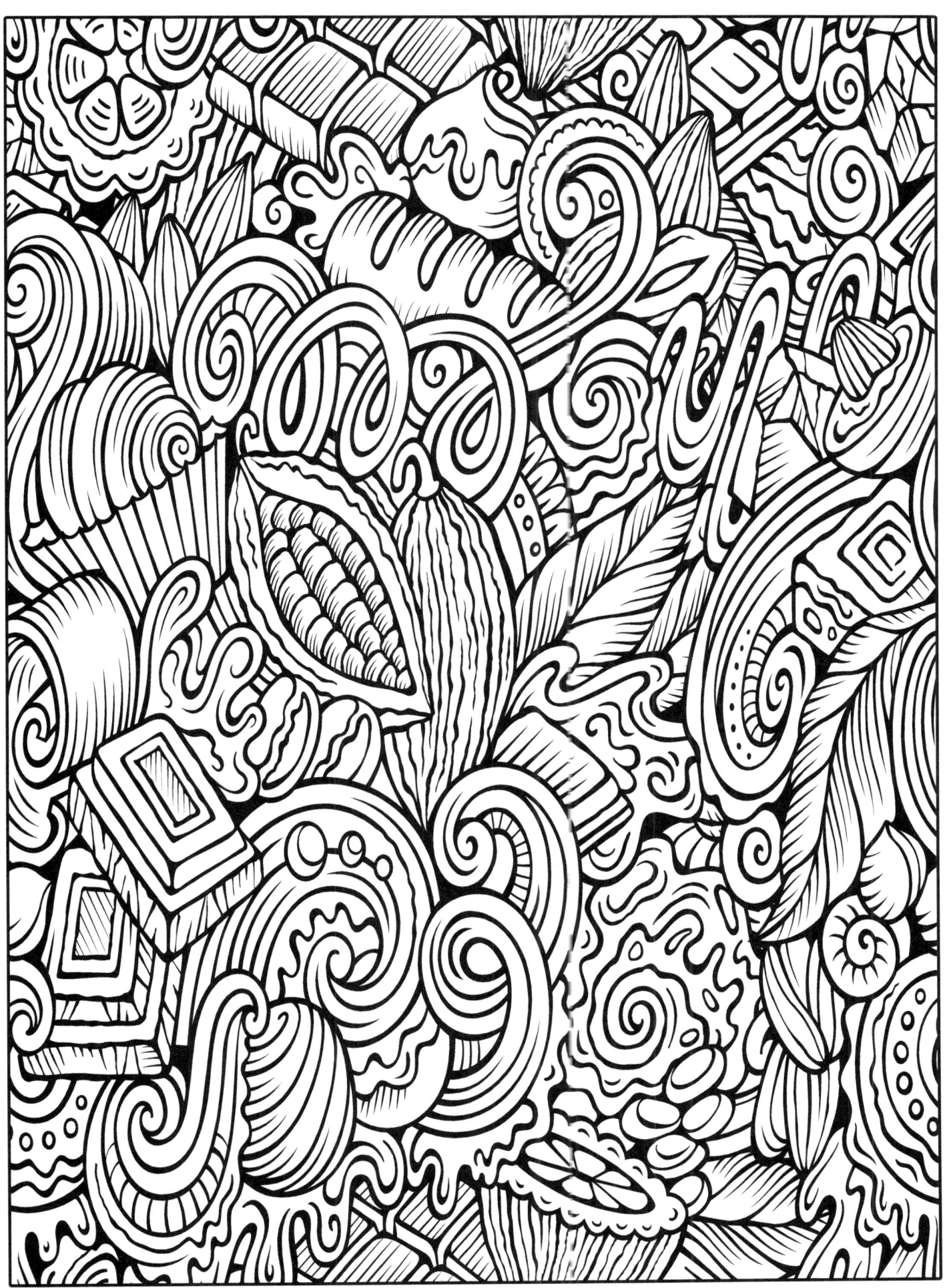

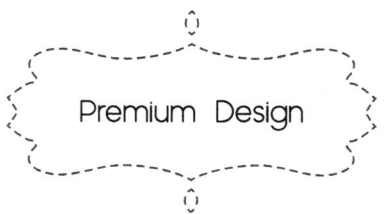

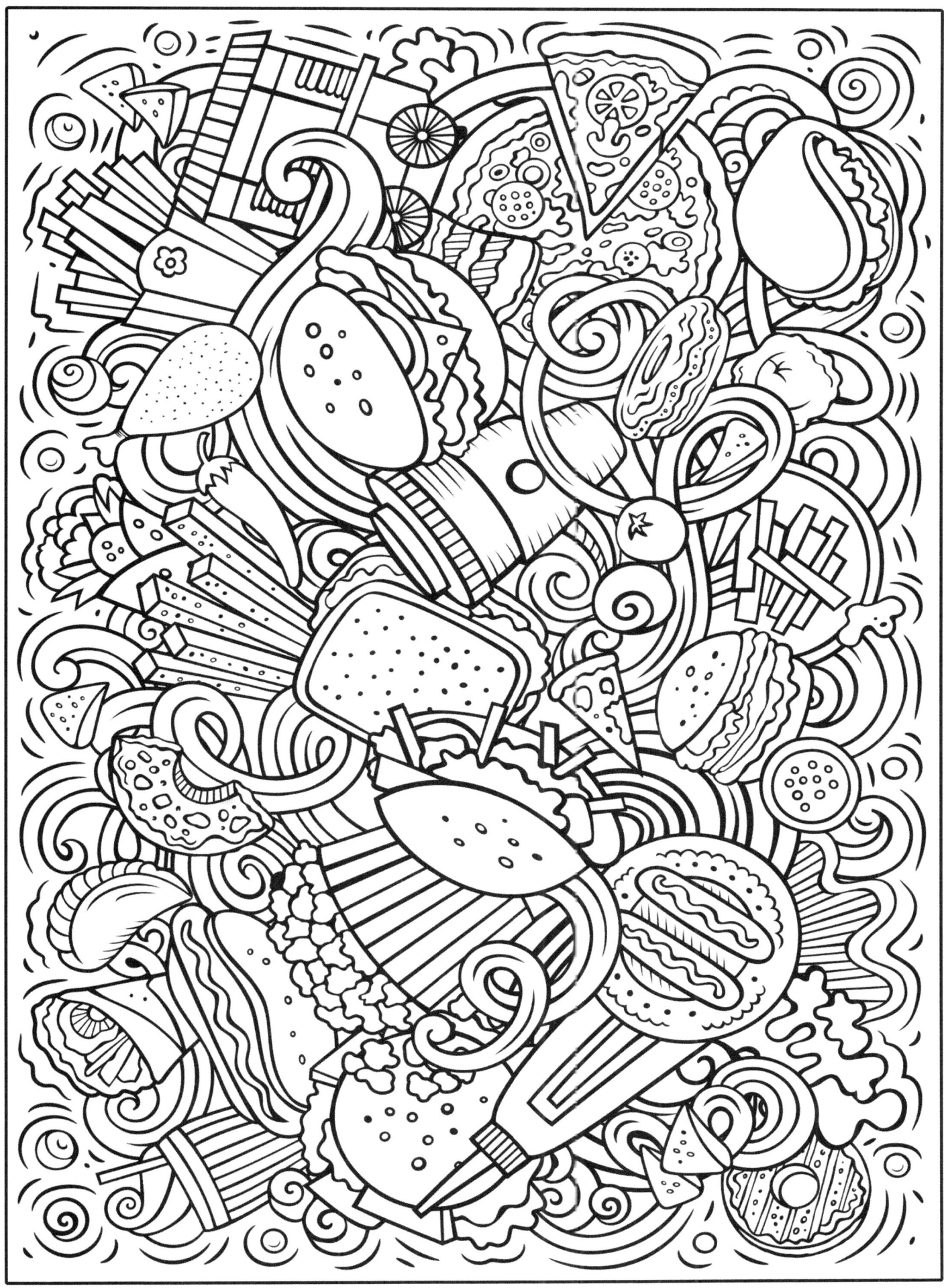

Premium Design

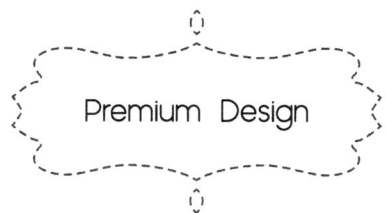

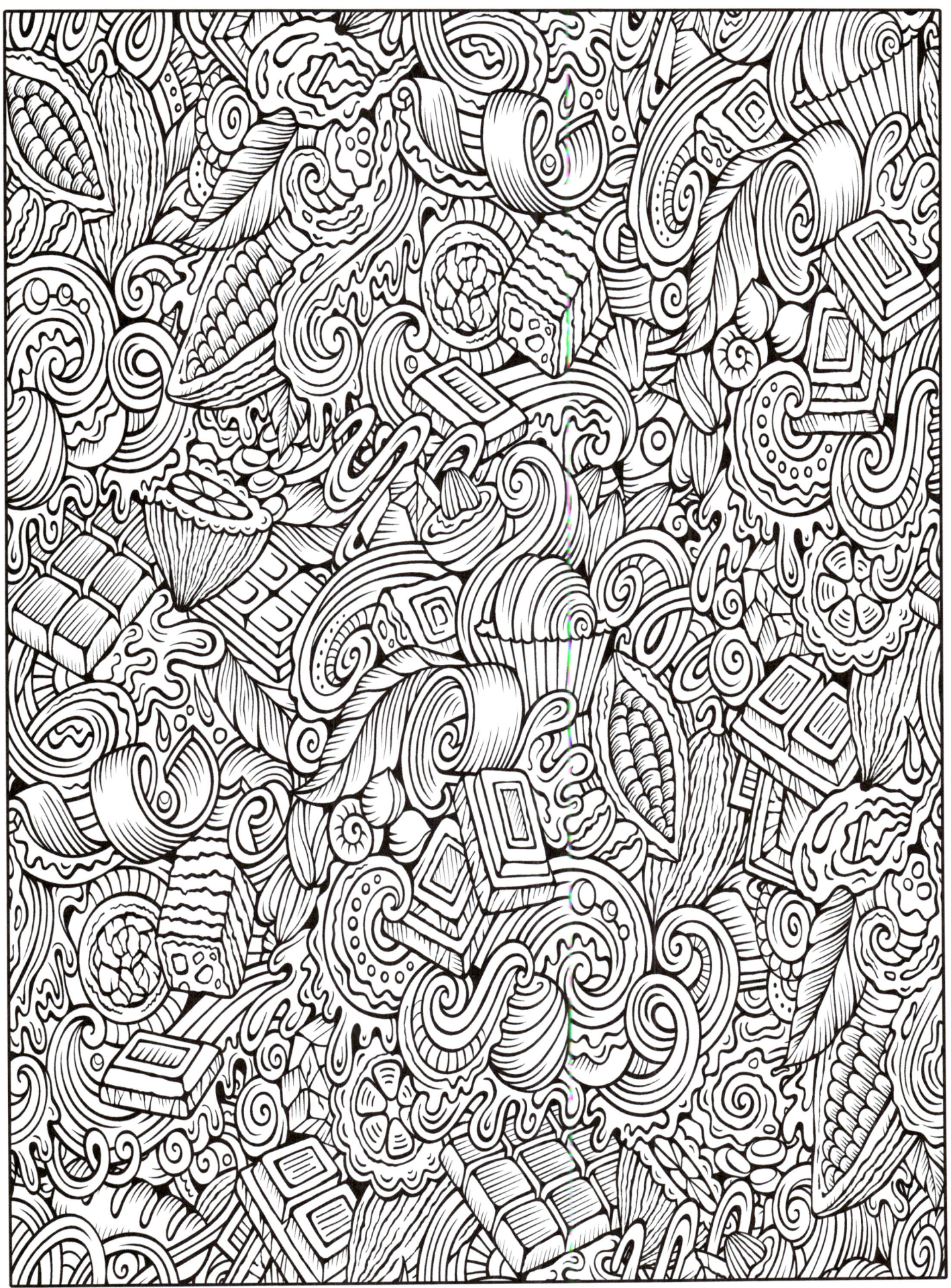

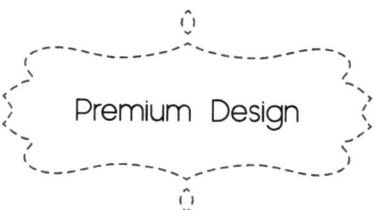

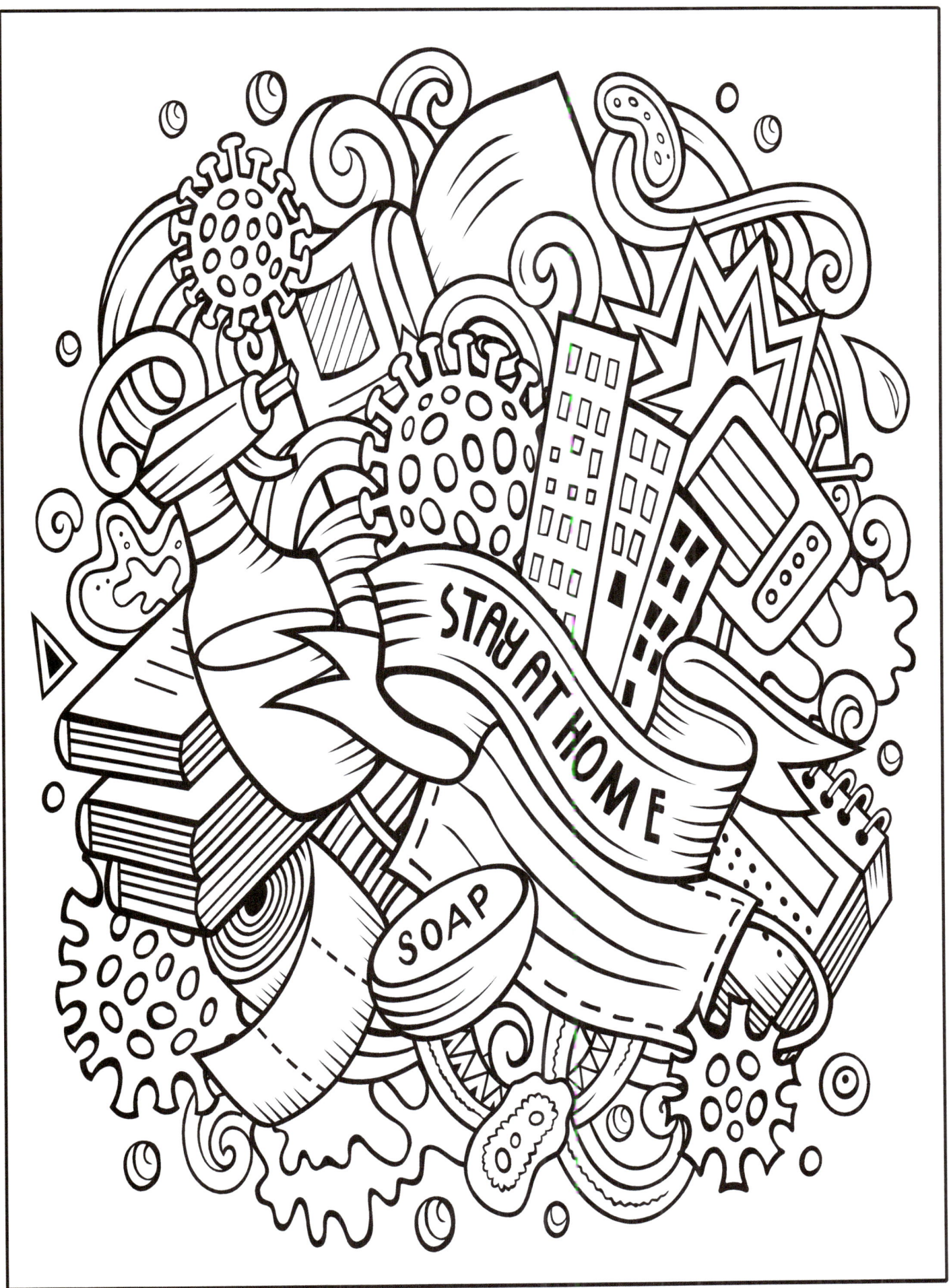

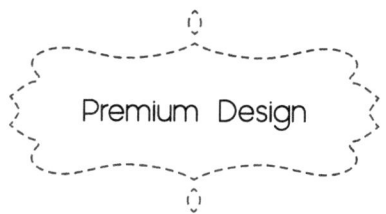

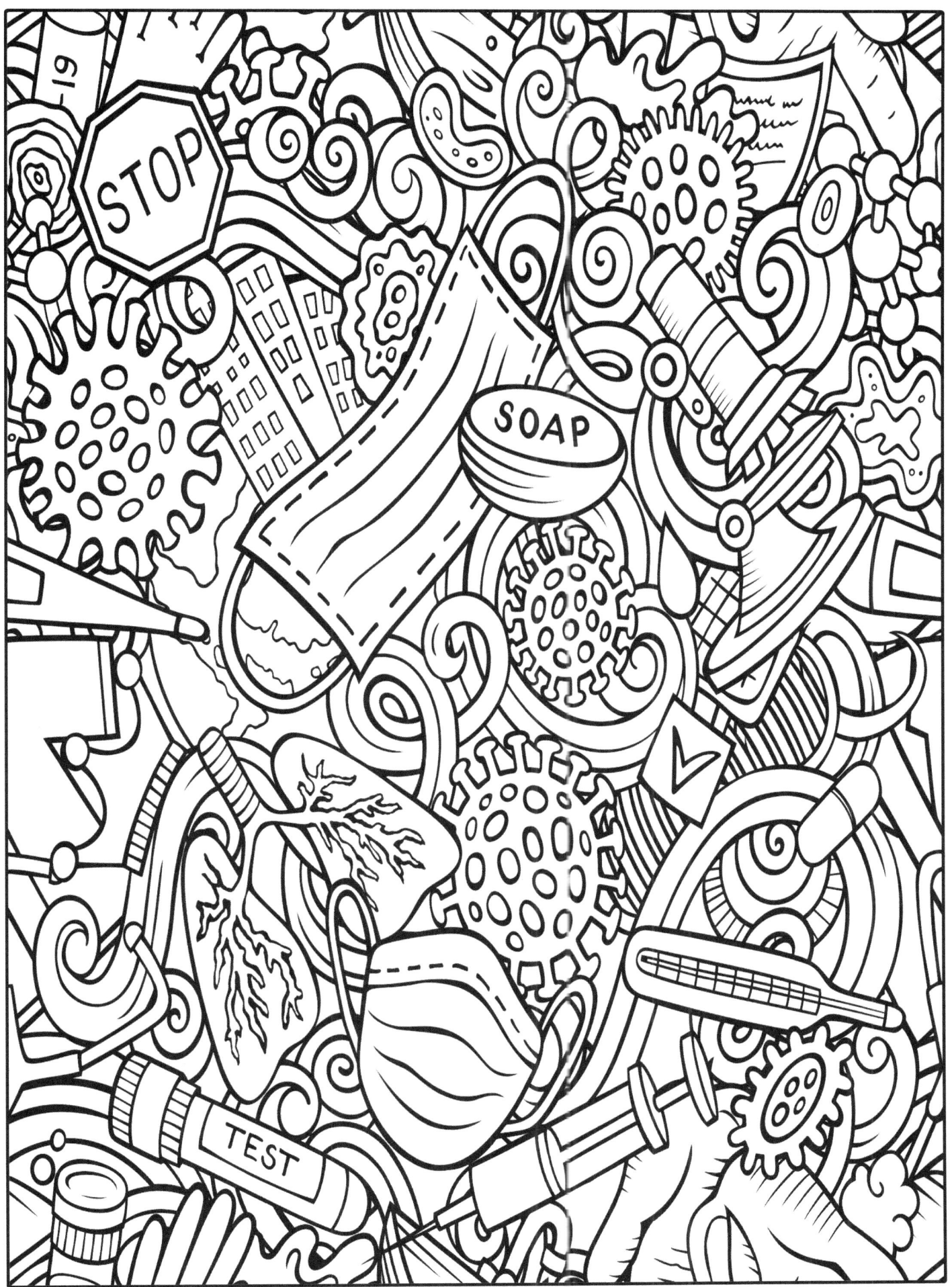

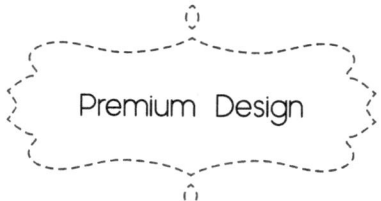

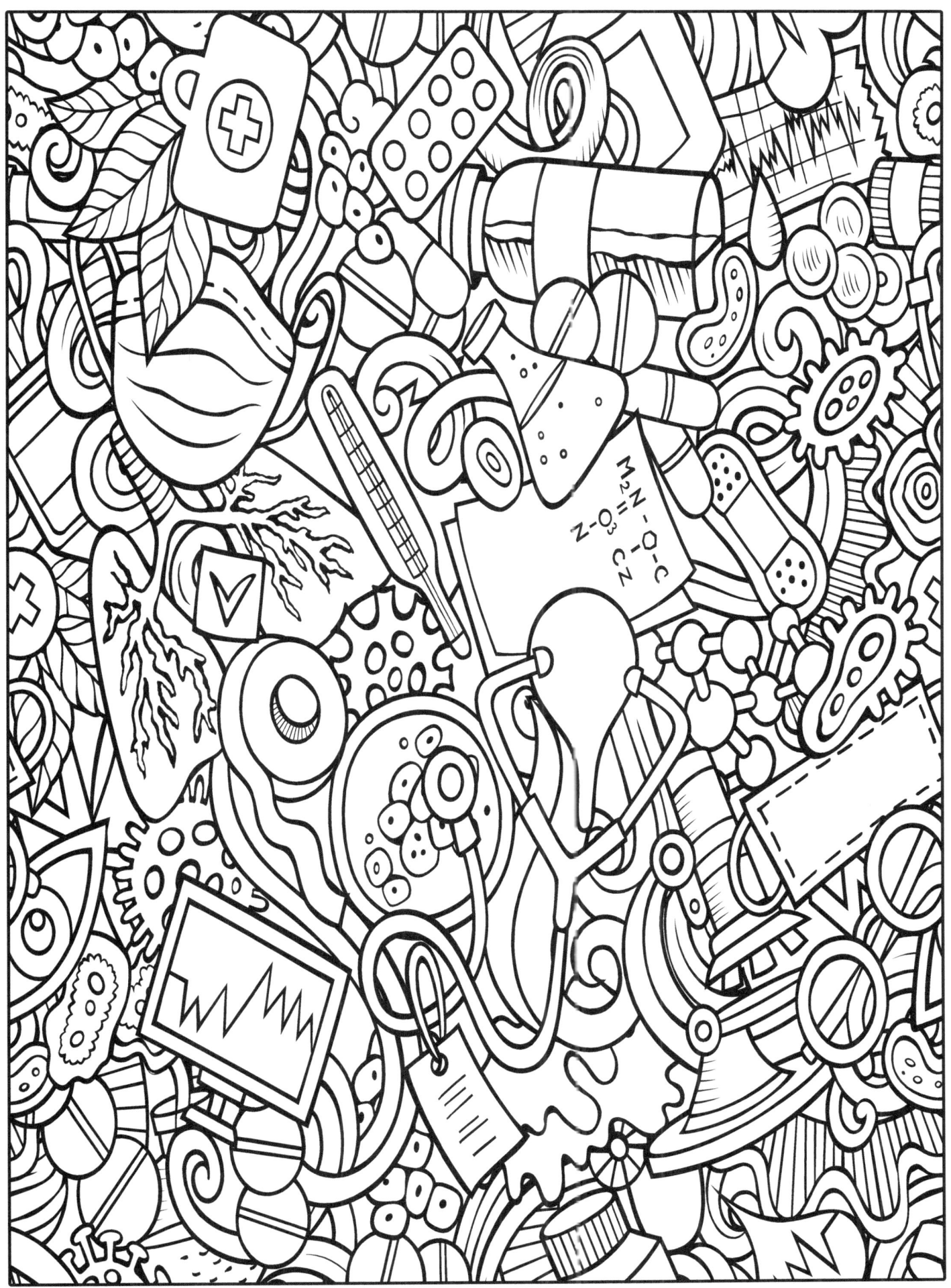

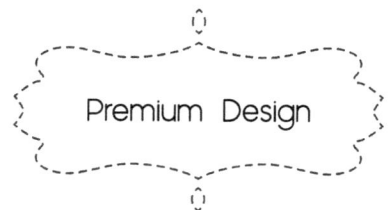

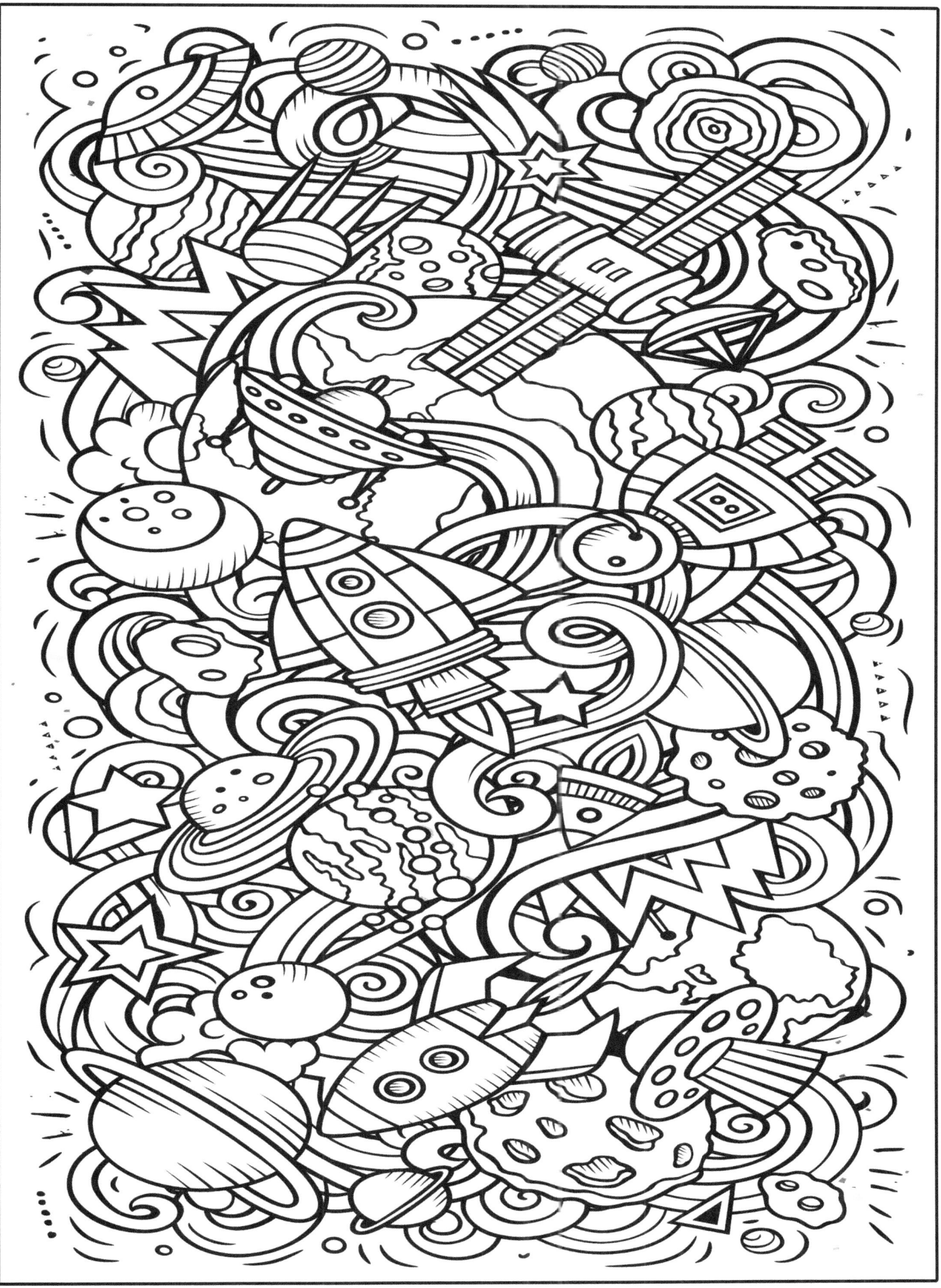

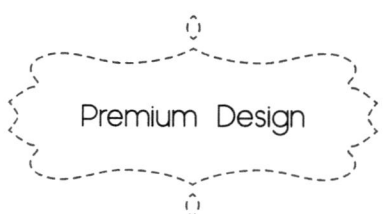

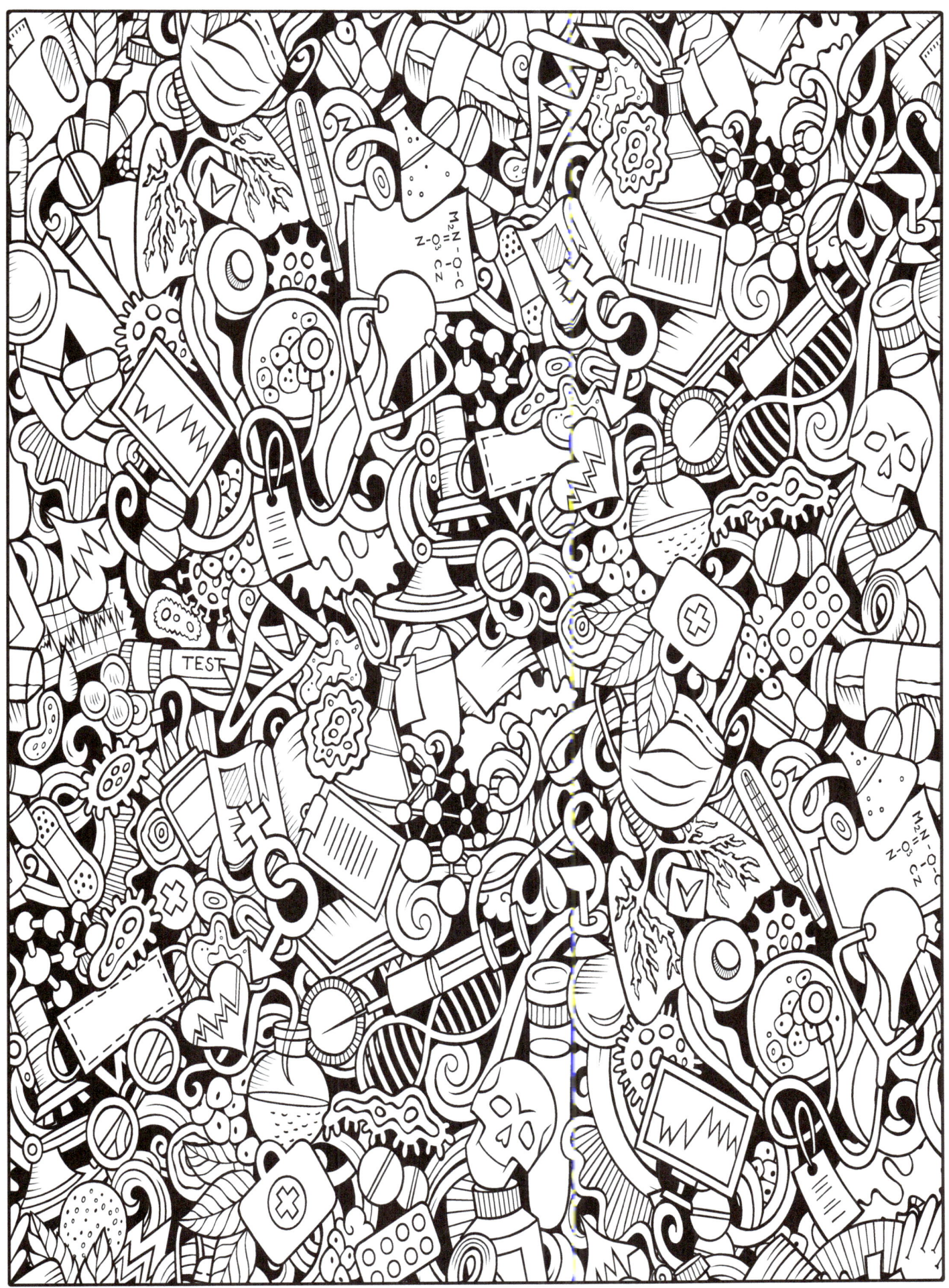

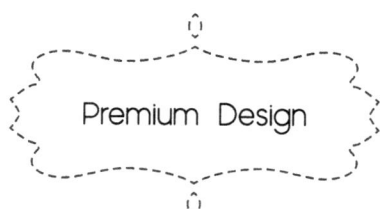

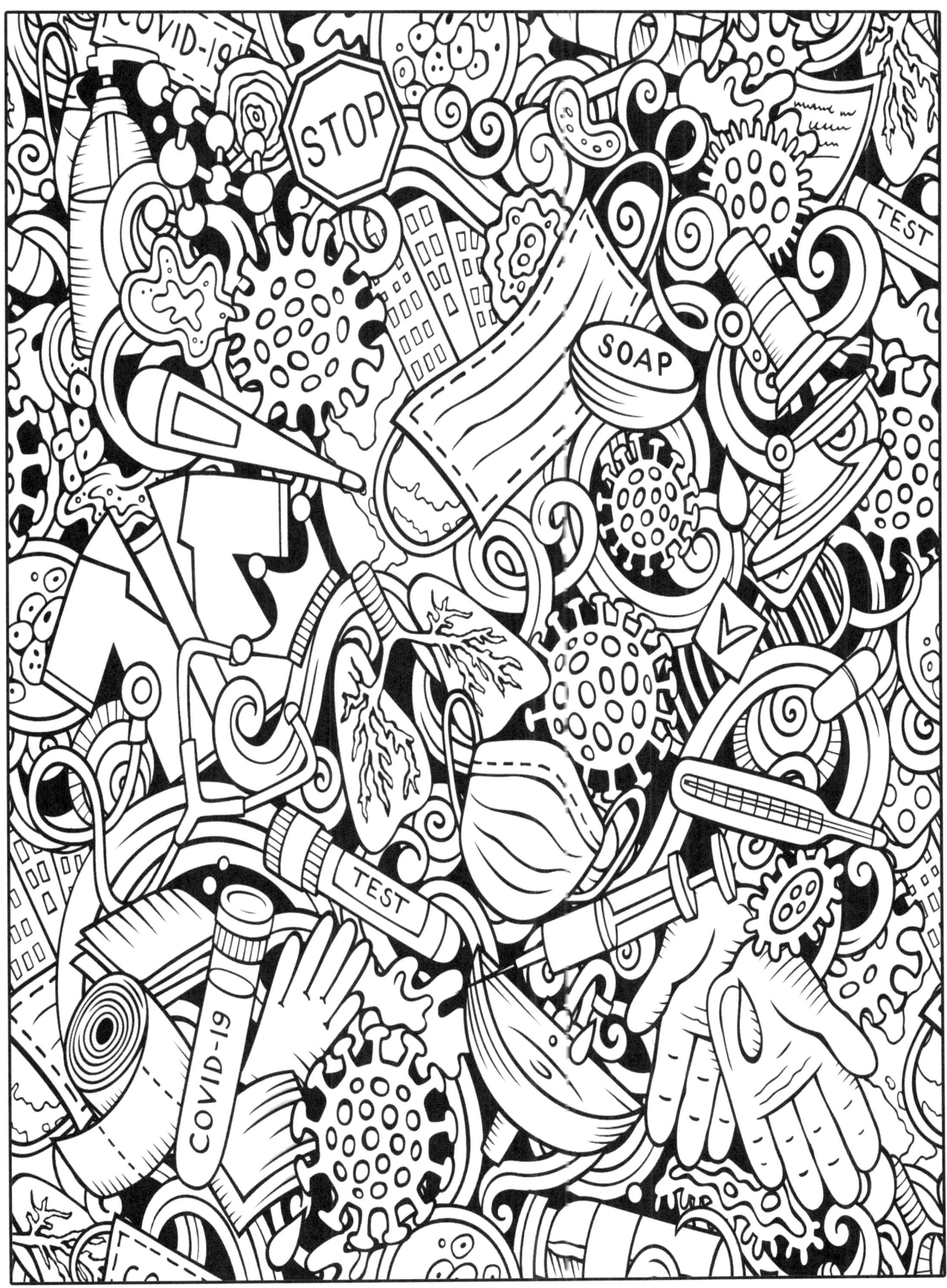

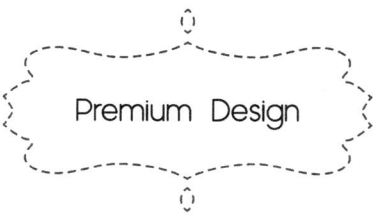

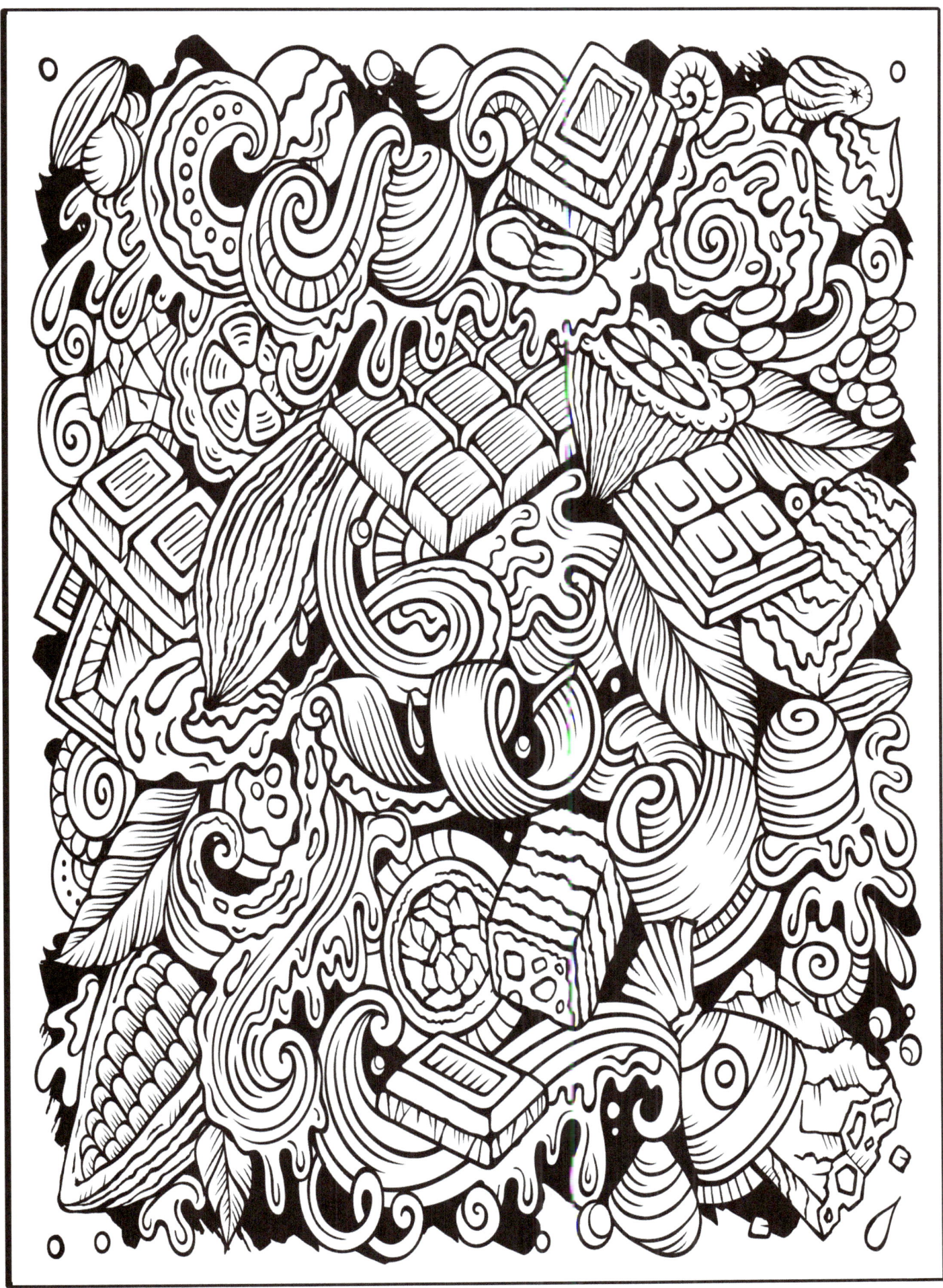

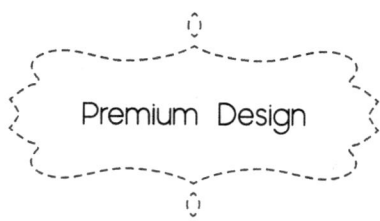

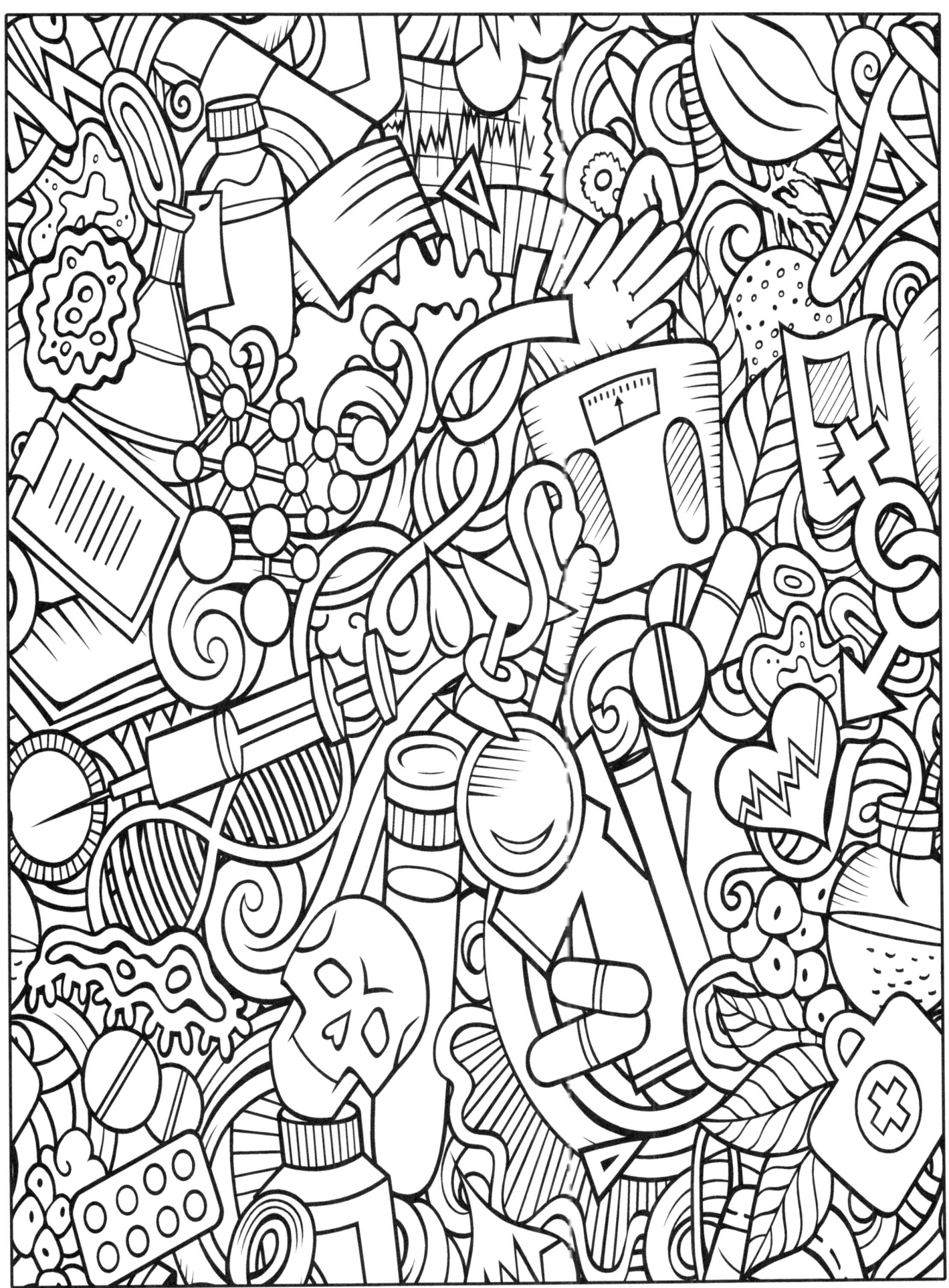

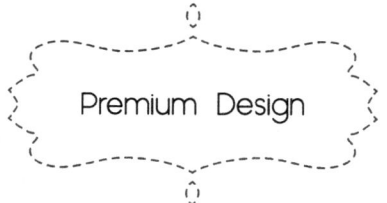

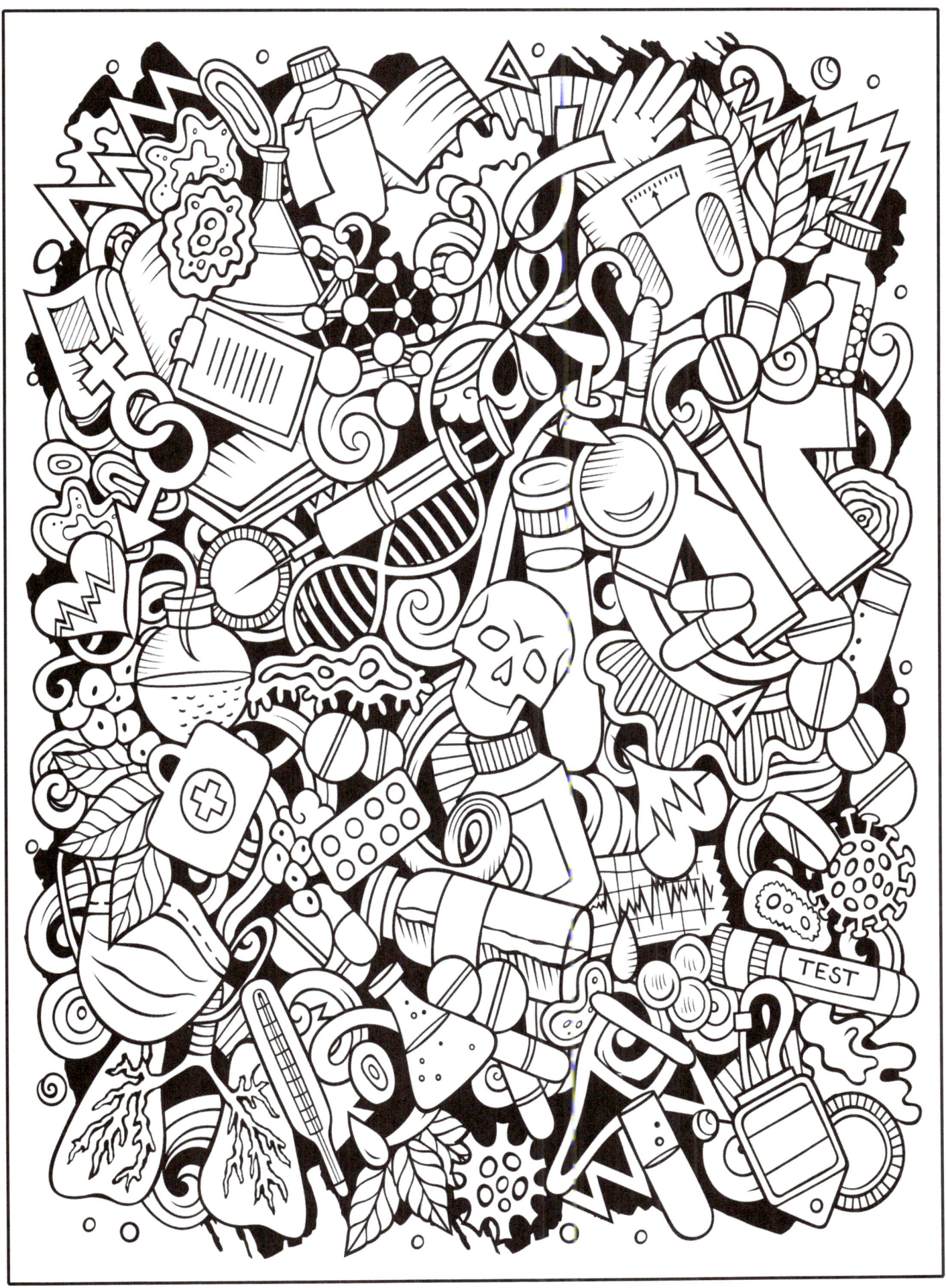

www.ingramcontent.com/pod-product-compliance
Lightning Source LLC
Chambersburg PA
CBHW060437220526
45465CB00008B/3179